W9-BCX-696

THE

THERMIDORIANS

THE

THERMIDORIANS

by

GEORGES

LEFEBVRE

Translated from the French by
ROBERT BALDICK

VINTAGE BOOKS
A Division of Random House
New York

4972

CONTENTS

FOREWORD

Albert Mathiez died on February 25, 1932, in his chair at the Sorbonne, where in spite of growing ill health he had insisted on giving his lecture at the usual time. He was only fifty-eight; his activity was greater than ever and his premature death deprived us of masterly works which he had been maturing for a long time. There is not one of his countless readers who is not aware of the irreparable loss suffered by French history.

Of all his undertakings, the one dearest to his heart was undoubtedly that history of the French Revolution of which he had already published three volumes. After taking it up to the ninth of Thermidor, he was getting ready to continue it. His book on the Thermidorian reaction, likewise published by Monsieur Jacques Max Leclerc, a work which sheds new light on many aspects of the history of that period, shows how carefully he had prepared, as always, for his next task. But he did not have time to begin the volume for which we were all waiting.

Like Monsieur Jacques Max Leclerc, the editor of the Collection Armand Colin felt that it would be regrettable to leave his work unfinished, and he invited me to continue it. When I accepted this invitation I did so with a full aware-

ness of the difficulty of the task, and I beg my readers to believe that if I undertook this task it was not in any spirit of
presumption. Nor was it with the intention of abdicating
my personal opinions in order to present nothing but a
pastiche. In agreement with the publisher and the editor of
the Collection, I simply felt that in continuing the work of
Albert Mathiez we should be paying his memory an homage
which would have pleased him.

GEORGES LEFEBVRE

NOTE: *This edition has been revised and corrected by
Albert Soboul.*

THE THERMIDORIANS

CHAPTER ONE

After the Ninth of Thermidor

On the ninth of Thermidor, France had been under a revolutionary regime, namely the dictatorship of the Committee of Public Safety, for about a year. The main question of the day was whether this regime would outlast Robespierre.

Brought into existence by the extreme danger in which the Revolution had found itself in 1793, the revolutionary government had restored to the executive the strength it had lacked since 1789: it had given it stability, the Committees of Public Safety and of General Security having been re-elected without any changes since September 1793;

3

it had restored centralization, all official appointments being made by the Committees or by their representatives on mission; and it had broken all resistance by means of the "coercive force" of the revolutionary courts, in other words by means of the Terror. Making full use of its authority, the Committee of Public Safety, for the first time in modern history, had organized a general mobilization of the national community, by proclaiming the *levée en masse* and obtaining control of the greater part of the economy, thanks to requisitioning and the *maximum*. Its efforts had been crowned with success: it had recaptured Lyons and Toulon; the Vendée insurrection was in its death-throes; the invasion had been repelled and the Republican armies had returned to the attack—since the victory of Fleurus they had been engaged in reconquering Belgium. However, the European Coalition remained in existence, and it was impossible even to envisage a time when a general peace might be concluded. Was this then a suitable moment to relax the grip of the revolutionary defense-system?

The Convention had no intention whatever of capitulating to the counterrevolution, but it felt a secret repugnance for the revolutionary government as it had functioned so far. Although—having suspended the application of the 1793 Constitution, and consequently the elections, until the end of hostilities—it had associated the Convention with its dictatorship, it was nonetheless not of parliamentary origin: the Montagnard minority had imposed it on the Assembly with outside help from the Jacobins gathered together in the popular clubs, and on the *sans-culottes*. To avoid being swept away by an insurrection, the Convention had been obliged to sacrifice the Girondins, accept the authority of the Committee of Public Safety, renounce any

4

sort of opposition, and hand over the Hébertists and the Dantonists. Now that the Committee of Public Safety, in splitting up, had called it in to arbitrate, and it had seized power again by outlawing the Robespierrists, its first thought could only be to defend its authority jealously, not only against the Jacobins of the clubs and the *sans-culottes* of the street, but also against such of its own members as it might appoint to govern in its name. For the moment the principle of dictatorship recommended itself; it was essential to complete the rout of the Robespierrists and suppress any fresh attempt at popular insurrection; besides, no assembly tends to consider its own powers excessive. But it was unthinkable that the Committee of Public Safety should be allowed to retain its stability and omnipotence, and with them the very essence of revolutionary government disappeared willy-nilly.

Even if events had worked out otherwise, that government would henceforth have been incapable of exacting obedience. It had succeeded in doing so only by imposing the Terror, which was bound to come to an end after the ninth of Thermidor. If the Terror had confined itself, as it should have, to punishing rebels and traitors, its swift and bloody repressive measures would still have aroused feelings of pity; as it turned out, during the last months of 1793, certain representatives on mission—Carrier at Nantes, Collot d'Herbois and Fouché at Lyons, Barras and Fréron at Toulon—in the fiery atmosphere of civil war, had allowed themselves to indulge in mass executions that were not always legal even under revolutionary law. The Committee of Public Safety had recalled them, but after regaining control of the repression, it had itself unleashed the great Terror in Paris, by the law of 22 Prairial, and had allowed Joseph Lebon and the Orange Commission to act with increasing severity. What is more, the Law of Suspects had enabled the revolutionary committees in a great many communes to take action, as against enemies of the Revolution, against a host of people whose birth, wealth or opinions marked them out for attack; religious conflicts, the process of dechristianization which the Committee had tried in vain to halt, and economic measures which only police surveillance could enforce, had extended the scope of repressive action even further; in short, the Jacobins had committed the supreme folly of attacking or alarming nearly everybody. Finally, the Terror had turned against the Republicans themselves: the *ultras* like the *citras*, the *enragés* and Hébertists like the Girondins and Dantonists, had all suffered from it; it was Babeuf who would soon be accusing the Committee of Public Safety of having turned it into a method of depopulating France. Once Robespierre had fallen, a tremendous movement of public opinion immediately turned against the Terror. The Convention could not forgive the latter for having decimated it, and Robespierre's colleagues themselves, by using it to blacken his memory, were the first to encourage a reaction. In reality the Terror did not really cease on the ninth of Thermidor any more than did the dictatorship; it was too much in the interests of the new rulers to turn it against their enemies, but it promptly ceased to sanction the essential measures of national defense—the *levée en masse*, requisitioning, the *maximum*—without which revolutionary government was just an empty phrase.

"Down with the terrorists!" immediately became the rallying cry of the Thermidorians, and countless voices repeated it, but not solely out of horror for bloodshed: it made it possible to conceal a movement of social reaction which lends the period its chief interest. In the opinion of the Jacobins and the *sans-culottes*, the need to defend the nation was not the sole justification for the revolutionary government; in rising to impose it on the Convention, the common people had also obeyed their own needs and their desire to modify the organization of society in order to profit, in their turn, from the Revolution. They suffered from unemployment, poverty, and the high prices created by inflation: the revolutionary government had at least provided them with bread at a reasonable price; it had given them work manufacturing armaments and had employed countless men on the surveillance committees and section committees as warders, keepers of the seals, and permanent National Guards; in Paris, "poor" citizens who attended both the decadal meetings of their section were paid forty sols each time. As the peasants clamored for land, either in order to become landowners or to round off their property, the national estates had been divided into small lots before being put up for sale, and certain facilities had been granted to impoverished citizens who wished to buy; a promise had been made to the "defenders of the country" that land to the value of a billion would be set aside for them; and then the decrees of Ventôse had announced that the property of "suspects" would be distributed free to indigent patriots. A free medical service had been instituted, national assistance guaranteed to old people without means and widows with dependent children, allowances granted to soldiers' relatives, and the right to compensation recognized for victims of war damage. In short, in exchange for the sacrifices which the revolutionary government imposed on the members of the national community, it had recognized their right to

7

life and had tried to turn this into a reality. *Sans-culottes* and Jacobins were not communists: artisans, shopkeepers, peasants, they were often property owners or, at any rate, asked for nothing better than to become property owners; the Montagnards, who came from the upper middle class, were even more hostile to socialism. But, apart from the fact that circumstances forced them to rely on the common people, they all had a sense of national solidarity and, like Rousseau, felt that political democracy was incompatible with an excessive inequality of wealth; in their eyes the "rich man" was suspect of disloyalty to the State, and was in fact often a counterrevolutionary or, at the very least, hostile to the Republic. Needing money, and needing it right away, the revolutionary government obtained it by forced loans and revolutionary taxes; it consolidated the authority of the National Debt by inscribing it in the Great Book and then reviewed life annuities; apart from the fact that the "enemies of the Revolution" were barred from holding Treasury scrip and were thus expropriated, the legal formalities, which often could not be observed in such circumstances, ruined a great many rentiers; moreover, dividends were held back and finally not paid at all. At the same time, new laws of succession insured the dissemination of inheritances, and the nationalization of a great part of the economy deprived the capitalist bourgeoisie of its usual profits: the armament contractors were eliminated, the bankers and merchants brought under control, the great financiers submitted to requisitioning. With their wealth thus threatened, the "notables" were also profoundly humiliated at losing the monopoly of public offices which the Constituent Assembly seemed to have promised them, and at finding themselves governed by members of the

8

lower middle class who had hitherto been their tenants and their tradesmen, or even by illiterate journeymen.

Consequently the attacks made on the terrorist were not directed simply at the "drinker of blood," nor even at the man who had dared to impose on everyone certain obligations which were considered unbearable (above all personal military service), but at the man who had undertaken to curb social individualism and to bar the way to a nascent capitalism; on this point the lower middle class, for the most part, joined in the chorus of blame, for while they distrusted the upper middle class, they had no desire to deprive themselves of the possibility of entering that class by fundamentally opposing it. Seen in this light, from the economic and social point of view, the Thermidorian reaction acquires an importance and an interest which are not usually recognized. Ostensibly it was a chaos of murderous political struggles in which the mutilated parties engaged only their dregs and which culminated in the crushing of the Jacobin minority, which, like the Thermidorians, is depicted as a rabble stained with crimes. In reality it eliminated democracy from the political and social life of France for nearly a century, renewed the link with the Revolution of 1789, and, with economic liberty and the electoral property qualification, began to establish that supremacy of the middle class which the Constituent Assembly had organized and which, at the end of the eighteenth century, seemed to be the supreme achievement of French history.

CHAPTER TWO

The Dismemberment of the Revolutionary Government

The committee members who had taken the initiative on
the ninth of Thermidor in order to save their necks had
imagined that at the same time they were consolidating
their authority; terrorists that they were, particularly Billaud-Varenne and Collot d'Herbois, they had no intention
of changing their methods in the slightest. Speaking on
their behalf on 10 Thermidor, Barère declared that the previous day had been merely "a slight commotion which left
the government untouched," and on the eleventh he presented three candidates to replace the three "conspirators"
Robespierre, Couthon and Saint-Just; from July to Septem-

ber, 1793, that was how, by a process of co-optation, the Committee of Public Safety of the Year II had gradually taken shape, the Convention confining itself to ratifying its choices. As Thibaudeau has put it, "the Committee of Public Safety was rid of Robespierre. The Convention was not rid of the Committee of Public Safety." But Barère's proposal led to a memorable debate which left the Convention with none of its illusions.

Merlin de Thionville gave the signal for attack with other Dantonists, Legendre and Thuriot, and with the turncoat terrorists, Bourdon de l'Oise and Tallien, who blamed the Committees for the policy with which they themselves had been associated for so long. It was doubtless too early to break with Robespierre's colleagues, but not to force them to share their power. "We have overthrown the triumvirs," exclaimed Tallien, "we do not want to replace them with decemvirs." This was how the Assembly felt too, and it made haste to regain power; besides, Barère himself had said: "The Convention is everything." It was decreed that a quarter of each Committee be replaced every month, and that retiring members be re-eligible only after an interval of one month. The stability of the government was in danger. For the moment, Barère, Billaud and Collot remained at their posts, but as it was decided to replace Jeanbon Saint-André, on the pretext that he was on mission, and also Hérault de Séchelles, who had been guillotined with Danton, half the Committee of Public Safety was renewed. On 13 Thermidor (July 31), Eschassériaux, one of Barère's candidates, was elected, together with the Dantonists Thuriot and Bréard, Treilhard who had voted for a stay of execution, Laloy whose brother and brother-in-law were reputed to be Royalists, and finally

Tallien. David, Lavicomterie and Jagot were excluded from the Committee of General Security as Robespierrists, and Merlin de Thionville was brought in, with Legendre, Bourdon's friend Goupilleau de Fontenay, and Dumont whose brother was a suspect. The personnel of the committees was thus modified to a significant extent.

It remained to be seen whether the Committee of Public Safety would retain at least the dominant position which had preserved the unity of the government. As early as the eleventh, Cambon had demanded that it be deprived of that position. During the whole of Year II, only one executive body had escaped from the authority of the Committee of Public Safety. This was the Treasury, which took its orders only from the Finance Committee, controlled by none other than Cambon himself; he proposed that the exception be made general, and that each of the twelve executive commissions which had taken the place of the ministries be put under the control of one of the Convention's twelve committees. On the thirteenth, Barère rushed into the breach and inveighed against the "moral federalism" which certain persons wished to institute; the Committee of Public Safety ought to retain the whip hand over the twelve executive commissions, and the Committee of General Security over the police; the other committees, as before, would have nothing to do but plan legislation. The Assembly hesitated, vaguely aware that it was dangerous to weaken the Executive by dividing it. But the fear of falling under the yoke once more won the day, and after lengthy debates the decree of 7 Fructidor (August 24) consecrated Cambon's proposal. Henceforth the Convention had sixteen committees, twelve of which were each in control of one of the executive commissions, with the right to issue decrees and dismiss officials. The Committee of Public Safety was left with nothing but war and foreign affairs; the Committee of General Security was confirmed in its control over the police; if both Committees retained the right to requisition troops, it was only through the mediation of the Military Committee. The Finance Committee retained its independence. The Legislative Committee was given responsibility for internal administration and justice; its importance was growing and it figured henceforth among what were generally called the "Three Committees." In short, the centralization of the government had disappeared.

On the other hand, with regard to the provinces, the Convention wanted to strengthen its central authority. On 1 Fructidor (August 18), speaking of the reform of the surveillance committees, Goupilleau de Fontenay declared: "We have started from the principle that the lawmakers entrusted with the task of leading the Revolution to its objective should themselves choose the elements intended to contribute to that aim." The central government therefore went on purging local administrations and completing them without having recourse to elections. As before the ninth of Thermidor, the Convention and its Committees sent representatives on mission, invested with more or less extensive powers, to the departments and to the armies; the Montagnards were recalled and generally replaced with moderates: this was the only innovation. Besides, the same mistrust was shown to them as by the Robespierrist Committees. On 26 Fructidor (September 12), Merlin de Douai criticized their independence and their tendency to legislate by means of decrees which were more often than not self-contradictory: "The legislation of the Republic has federalized itself in the strangest way." They were instructed to send their decrees to the Committees, which could annul them. Already all the representatives sent into the departments had been recalled on the twelfth (August 29); the missions had been restricted to six months for the armies and three for the interior, with a ban on any fresh mission before an interval of three months. In reality, the situation changed scarcely at all. Distance, the slowness of communications, and urgency made it necessary to give great latitude to the representatives on mission; like their predecessors, each had his own personal policy according to his temperament, his ideas and his prejudices; ignorant of local conditions or overburdened with work, they allowed themselves to be guided by local political leaders: the only difference was that usually the Jacobins, who until then had more often than not advised the members of the Convention, henceforth saw them listening only to their enemies. It was therefore in vain that the Thermidorian majority showed its intention of strengthening the system of centralization for its own advantage; it had actually weakened it by destroying the unity of the government.

The public did not care about these problems. It was overjoyed at seeing the repression on the wane; in the Convention itself, the organization of the government caused very little excitement, whereas the slightest reference to the Terror provoked an uproar. On 11 Thermidor, Barère had insisted on maintaining the Terror as "the order of the day": "There can be no indulgence except for involuntary errors; but the aristocrats' intrigues are offenses and their errors are crimes." In reality, the "coercive force," one of the essential elements of the revolutionary government, disappeared at the same time as the others. The revolutionary court had ceased to function, its president, Dumas, and several of the jurymen having been guillotined; Fouquier-Tinville and Herman, who had directed the commission of civil cases, were in prison; and the two commissions entrusted with the task of sorting out suspects—the only commissions set up under the decrees of Ventôse—having been deprived of their presidents who had likewise been arrested, suspended their activities and never resumed them. The terrorists wanted this crisis to come to an end; while admitting the need to purge the revolutionary court, Barère had called for "great respect" to be shown to that "salutary institution"; Goupilleau de Fontenay said the same of the revolutionary Committees. But there seems to be no doubt that, in order to carry the Plain with them, they had promised it to modify the law; besides, they threw the responsibility for the Great Terror onto Robespierre and the law of 22 Prairial. This latter law was hated by the Convention because, so it was thought, it allowed the Committees to send deputies before the revolutionary court without consulting the Assembly. It was repealed on 14 Thermidor (August 1). On the twenty-third (August 10), when Merlin de Douai reorganized the revolutionary court, whose president was Dobsen, the man of the thirty-first of May, Bourdon obtained an assurance that in the case of every convicted person the jury would examine the question of motive, and thanks to this decisive clause the court lost no time in releasing a great many convicted prisoners, on the pretext that they had not intended to help the counterrevolution.

In the meantime, all executions having been suspended, attention had been turned to the prisons. From the Hébertists to the Dantonists, there was not a single Republican clique which did not have some of its members behind bars. Having regained some of their former influence, the deputies' first thought was to use it on behalf of their friends; Tallien, who complained about this on 22 Thermidor (August 9), himself moved heaven and earth to obtain the release of his mistress, Thérèse Cabarrus, the former Marquise de Fontenay. Bentabole and Rovère, who married respectively Madame de Chabot and the Marquise d'Agoult, probably had no lack of clients either. As early as the tenth, Barère had promised that the Committees would examine the case of "patriots" in detention, and commissioners were sent to the prisons for this purpose. "There is not a single man in prison today," said Tallien, "who does not claim to be an ardent patriot and who has not been an enemy of Robespierre's." Between 18 Thermidor and 23 Thermidor, 478 people were released.

However inclined it was towards indulgence, the Convention found right away that its hands were not entirely free. Once again, pressure was exerted on it from outside; in the past, the Terror had been imposed on it; now it was required to abolish it, pending a demand for a terror in reverse. To begin with, public opinion seemed unanimous. The Jacobin Club, which Billaud and Legendre had gone together to reopen on 11 Thermidor, called for the release of a great many of its former members. Similarly the Sections protested at their meetings on 15 Thermidor (August 2), the first they had held since Robespierre's death. In Fructidor some provincial delegations, from Nîmes and Lyons, made their appearance. On 18 Thermidor (August 15), the Convention had satisfied a fundamental requirement by ordering the release of those suspects against whom no charge had been brought and by decreeing that henceforth the accusations made against prisoners should be communicated to them. On the twenty-ninth, the decree of 21 Messidor which had restored the farm workers to freedom was extended to communes with over 1,200 inhabitants, and liberal use was made of it with the aid of forged certificates.

Calling for the release of suspects amounted to saying that the surveillance committees had arrested them unjustly; consequently a simultaneous attack was launched on these committees. At their meetings on 15 Thermidor, certain Sections had decided to examine their operations; on the twenty-fifth (August 12) the Panthéon Section declared that its revolutionary committee had lost its confidence and the Montreuil Section denounced its own to the Convention. Cambon joined the attackers for economic reasons, since the members of these committees were paid five livres a day; during the course of the autumn he would go on to support the accusations promptly leveled at their integrity, maintaining that they had fraudulently converted some of the silver from the churches and some of the revolutionary taxes. Already, on 7 Fructidor (August 24), the Convention had given way. On a motion put forward by Goupilleau de Fontenay, it agreed that the surveillance committees were too numerous to be supervised themselves, and left only one in each district; its members were to resign every three months and would not be re-eligible until the expiration of a similar period; they were to be able to read and write, could issue a warrant for arrest only on a majority vote, and had to send the relevant file to Paris within twenty-four hours. The forty-eight Sections in the capital were grouped into twelve arrondissements (this was the origin of this territorial subdivision which lasted until 1860) and each four Sections were left with only one committee, which was of course nominated by the Committee of General Security; at the beginning, shopkeepers and artisans continued to predominate on these committees, but it was not long before "respectable folk" were in the majority.

It was in the provinces above all that the decree of 7 Fructidor caused a sensation, for it dealt a mortal blow to Jacobin supremacy. Changing all the local administrations was an extremely lengthy task; besides, in many departments the new representatives on mission did not arrive until the autumn. On the other hand the decree of 7 Fructidor affected the surveillance committees right away: most of them disappeared, while the others were reconstituted and ceased to act outside their residences. Now it was they who had put the Law of Suspects into application and had become the chief purveyors to the revolutionary courts. There were few places where anybody had dared to lay hands on them, as at Nîmes where the district had had Mayor Courbis and fifteen of his friends arrested on 20 Thermidor (August 7). Consequently the Terror had often continued after the ninth of Thermidor. On the thirteenth (July 31) the Convention had suspended the Popular Commission at Orange, but on the same day, at Brest, the revolutionary court sent General Moreau's father to the guillotine. In the Ardèche, on the eighteenth (August 5), five priests and three nuns were executed. At Château-Gontier, the Huchedé Commission began its operations on 9 Thermidor (July 27) and continued them during August. Admittedly the pressure of public opinion increased the number of acquittals; all the same, there were very few releases before Fructidor: at Dreux the first were on August

20, at Verdun in September, at Brest in October. It was after the decree of 7 Fructidor that the Terror really vanished.

Nevertheless, thanks to the slowness of the purge, the Jacobins remained influential for a long time on administrative bodies. Where the Terror had been particularly violent, the reaction was often immediate, for example at Bourg where Boisset had been sent at once, at Avignon where Rovère had sent his friend Goupilleau de Montaigu, and at Marseilles where Auguis and Serre started operations. But in the Seine-Inférieure, the municipality of Rouen was purged only on 6 Vendémiaire, Year III (September 27, 1794) and the department only on 5 Frimaire (November 25); the Hérault, the Ardennes and the Mayenne were affected only in Brumaire, the Haute-Saône, the Ardèche, the Ariège and the district of Dinan in Frimaire, and the Manche in Nivôse; the municipality of Reims remained intact until 7 Germinal (March 27, 1795), that of Vire until 23 Floréal (May 12), and the same was true, with all the more reason, of the little communes. What is more, many representatives, such as Berlier in the Nord and Perrin in the Bas-Languedoc, tried to curb the reaction; at Nîmes, Perrin picked moderate Montagnards from the middle class, for example Bonicel, Guizot's maternal grandfather, and actually formed the surveillance committee out of artisans and laborers. The technique was to distinguish between the agitators and the Republicans they had led astray. It even happened that, in the Meurthe, Michaud restored to office the *sans-culottes* who had been imprisoned as Hébertists before the ninth of Thermidor.

The fact remains that once the institutions of Year II

had been condemned, the terrorist leaders and particularly the members of the former surveillance committees could not help being called to account. In Paris, a great many Jacobins who had been compromised in the events of the ninth of Thermidor had been imprisoned. On 15 Thermidor (August 2), Lebon had been placed under arrest; the day before, the terrorists of Sedan had suffered the same fate. Several representatives on mission imitated the Convention: Boisset, at Bourg, had the terrorists of 24 Thermidor (August 11) arrested; at Saint-Étienne, Reverchon imprisoned Pignon, the prosecutor of the criminal court; on 17 Fructidor (September 3), Goupilleau incarcerated the members of the Orange Commission; at Nîmes, the district had taken the initiative; at Bordeaux, Ysabeau actually set up a commission with instructions to review the revolutionary judgments.

In Fructidor, several provincial delegations started denouncing at the bar of the Convention certain former representatives on mission—Mallarmé on the seventh and Maignet on the eighth—with the support of Guffroy, Rovère and Fréron, who were prompted by a fanatical hatred of their personal enemies. Henceforth the noose promptly tightened around the terrorists on the government committees. In striking down Robespierre, writes Thibaudeau, "they had passed sentence on themselves. They would have liked to make him their scapegoat, so as to be able to blame all the past on him. But it was not a question of secret acts with which they could easily load his memory without fear of contradiction. The facts were public and patent." Billaud, Collot and Barère were the targets at this time. The journalists began to give voice. On 20 Thermidor (August 7), in *La Correspondance politique*, Dusaulx, addressing Fréron, cried: "Remember that you have ghosts to avenge!" How could Danton be avenged without Billaud being attacked? There was nothing left to protect the initiators of the ninth of Thermidor but the fragile alliance which had united them on that day with the turncoat terrorists—now in their turn ready to sacrifice them in order to save themselves—and with the moderates who hated them. Their friends finally broke that alliance by trying to take the initiative once more.

They had good reason to feel alarmed. There were plenty of indications that, now the Terror had come to an end, the government was no longer obeyed. The refractory conscripts or deserters no longer made any attempt at concealment; the peasants began to hold back their grain; the *maximum* was openly flouted; some émigrés had returned—at the news of the ninth of Thermidor, Doulcet de Pontécoulant had left Switzerland; and here and there, churches were reopened by force. In the provinces the Jacobins raised the alarm, but as their friends had no remedy to propose but a return to the Terror, they came up against insurmountable repugnance among the public. On 23 Thermidor (August 10), Granet, protesting at the release of the suspects, succeeded in getting the names of those who were released and of their guarantors published. Merlin de Thionville, Legendre and Tallien saw this as an attack on themselves. On the twenty-sixth, namely the very day that Tallien's mistress was released, they launched a violent attack on the decree of the twenty-third. Meeting a lively show of resistance, Tallien cunningly obtained the passing of a decree that the names of the denouncers should also be published. It was the terrorists' turn to tremble: this was civil war, they cried. Tallien agreed and frankly explained the purpose of his maneuver, which was crowned with success, for Amar proposed and obtained the repeal of both decrees. On 2 Fructidor (August 19), the debate took a wider turn. Louchet, the very man who had issued the official charge against Robespierre, described the progress of the reaction, called for the reincarceration of the suspects, and declared that it was essential to "keep the Terror as the order of the day." A great shout of "Justice! Justice!" interrupted him. Tallien revealed himself openly as a right-wing orator: "The Terror is the work of tyranny. . . . I recognize no more castes in the Republic, only good and bad citizens." On the eleventh (August 28), he added that henceforth it was justice which would be the order of the day. He had thus sounded the rallying cries which would cover all reactionaries including even the Royalists. Two days before, Fréron had added that of the freedom of the Press, which, he said, did not exist unless it was absolute. Passions promptly rose to boiling point. As disasters followed one after another—on 3 Fructidor (August 20), the great saltpeter factory at L'Abbaye was destroyed by fire, and on the fourteenth the powder factory at Grenelle blew up—the terrorists saw the hand of the suspects in these events. Their enemies replied in the newspapers, and on the ninth (August 26), Méhée de la Touche published a pamphlet against them which soon became famous: *La Queue de Robespierre*.

Three days later, on 12 Fructidor, Lecointre took it upon himself to accuse Barère, Billaud and Collot, in the Convention itself, of having participated in "the tyranny," as well as Vadier, Amar, Voulland and David, of the Committee of General Security. Challenged to produce his evidence, he had to admit that he had none. Tallien abandoned him and, on a motion put by Cambon, the Assembly condemned the slanderous accusation. But it still had its effect: on the fifteenth (September 1), Barère, Billaud and Collot resigned from the Committee of Public Safety. It had taken little more than a month for the men of Year II, once they had abandoned Robespierre, to lose the "levers of power." In the Convention, the Mountain, which was given the derisive nickname of the Crest, reduced by daily defections, and led by second-rate men such as Duhem, Goujon and Fayau, lost all influence; Barère, Collot and Billaud had to give up speaking.

In spite of its successes, the Right did not take power. Along with Barère, Billaud and Collot, the turncoat terrorists who directed it—Fouché, Barras and Fréron—were removed from the Committees. Tallien himself, compromised by Lecointre, left the Committee of Public Safety. Rovère wrote to his friend Goupilleau that Tallien and Fréron could no longer count on more than 150 deputies. The majority in the Convention consequently lay in the Center, in the so-called Plain, reinforced by converts from the Mountain and by turncoat terrorists like Bourdon, who were opposed to an extreme reaction. In this majority, Merlin de Douai and Cambacérès occupied an eminent place; moreover, the new members of the committees were all chosen from among the regicides. It is in these men of the Center, represented for us by Thibaudeau, that the spirit of the Thermidorian Convention and indeed of the Convention as a whole is really incarnate. Their loy-

23

alty to the Revolution and to the Republic was never in doubt for a moment: on 3 Brumaire, Year III (October 24, 1794), they excluded the deputy Chabot because the primary assembly of Montluçon, which had elected him on August 26, 1792, had given its representatives a mandate to uphold the monarchy; on 25 Brumaire (November 15), they would maintain and codify the laws passed against the émigrés; exiled priests would remain liable to the death penalty if they returned to France. With regard to the constitutional priests, these Thermidorian Republicans were scarcely less hostile than the *sans-culottes*, and on the second *jour sans-culottide* (September 18, 1794), on a motion put forward by Cambon —as usual on the lookout for economies—they suppressed the religious estimates.

But they belonged to the middle class; they wanted to give the businessman his freedom back and reduce the poor man once more to a subordinate position. They were deputies and, jealous of their authority, they feared the dictatorship of the mob more than anything else. Consequently they wanted to avoid at all costs falling once more under the yoke of the Jacobins, who were terrorists and partisans of a social democracy. Realizing however that if they divided, the Republicans risked losing everything, their policy was to grant a tacit amnesty to the men of Year II, with the exception of those who might be convicted of illegalities or of common-law crimes, in order to reconcile all the "patriots of 1789" for the defense of the Revolution.

This was the program which Berlier, among others, put forward from the start in the Nord, in order to hold back the reaction; the committees, for their part, would try during the autumn, by means of their calculated slowness, to prevent the outlawing of the terrorist leaders.

But, as in 1793, the decisive step was not taken by the Conventional majority: the decision came from outside. And as the enemies of the Jacobins had been able to gain control of the mob, it was they who dictated it.

CHAPTER THREE

Jacobin Activity

Encouraged by Lecointre's reverse, the Mountain made an effort to regain the initiative. At the Jacobin Club, Lecointre, Tallien and Fréron, attacked by Carrier, were expelled on 17 Fructidor (September 3). On the twenty-first, Duhem obtained a decision to examine the means of carrying out "the prompt export of the sworn enemies of the Republic," in other words the deportation of the suspects, although several members had argued that this was a hopeless demand and that it was unwise to affront public opinion in this way. At the same time a few provincial clubs which had remained loyal to their mother-society admonished the Convention. The most violent petition was that of the Jacobins of Dijon: it called for the application of the Law of Suspects, the exclusion of nobles and priests from all public offices, and reconsideration of the decree on the question of motive; and it declared that until peace was concluded absolute freedom of the press was inadmissible. Up to 10 Vendémiaire, Year III (October 1, 1794), the Correspondence Committee of the Convention almost daily analyzed similar documents, mainly from the southeast (Lyons, Marseilles, Aix, Toulon, Manosque, Grenoble) and from the Languedoc (Toulouse, Montpellier, Cette), but also from Rennes, Poitiers, Auxerre, and little towns such as Aigueperse, Creuilly and Richelieu. On the third *jour sans-culottide* (September 19), the mother-society addressed a circular to all the affiliated clubs, obviously in the hope of widening the scope of the movement.

It was undoubtedly in order to rally the *sans-culottes* that some Montagnards suddenly began to display a remarkable enthusiasm for social reform. On 22 Fructidor (September 8), Duquesnoy complained that, in the Pas-de-Calais, national property had been monopolized by the rich, and Fayau proposed a return to the law of June 3, 1793, which had granted one acre to citizens who owned no land, in return for a yearly rental and without requiring them to attend the auction sale; he also demanded that the share which had been promised to the defenders of the country should be handed over to them immediately. Barère went further: he spoke of fixing a *maximum* for landed property, and asked that shops and workshops be made over to the workers.

It is just possible that these proposals had a slight echo

in Paris. The terrorists had made an effort, and not without success, to regain control of the Section meetings. As only a small number of citizens normally attended these meetings, it was not difficult for a few determined men—Jacobins or counterrevolutionaries—to get their motions passed, especially at the end of the meeting, when most of those present had gone home to bed. Be that as it may, at the meetings held on 20 and 30 Fructidor (September 6 and 16), at least eight Sections gave their support to the petition from the Dijon club. Two symbolic events made a considerable impression on public opinion and seemed to indicate a return to the Terror: on 26 Fructidor (September 12), the new revolutionary court condemned a wigmaker to death for making royalist remarks, and on the same day the Convention agreed to the transfer of Marat's body to the Panthéon, where it was taken on the fifth *jour sans-culottide* (September 21).

In matters of substance, the Thermidorian majority nonetheless showed a firm determination not to follow the terrorists. The releases continued: between 23 Thermidor and 16 Vendémiaire, 3,615 releases were ordered, which incidentally still left 4,678 people imprisoned in Paris. On 10 Vendémiaire, Year III (October 1, 1794), the Committee of General Security was authorized to decide on the sentences of detention until the conclusion of peace pronunced by the revolutionary courts. On the other hand, when on 25 Fructidor (September 11) the Jacobins, who had been violently denounced the day before by Merlin de Thionville, presented an address in favor of the patriots in prison, it was buried by being referred to the Committees. Legal action against the terrorists was begun. On 7 Fructidor, Ruelle had asked in vain that the new members of the revolutionary committees be forbidden to have their predecessors arrested: on 12 Vendémiaire (October 3), Bourdon announced among other arrests that the former committee of the Bonnet Rouge Section had been incarcerated for having falsified its minute-book. On the seventh (September 28), Cambacérès had pushed through an important decree to accelerate the purge of the administrative bodies. The social measures proposed by the Mountain had been set aside on 27 Fructidor (September 13) with the help of Cambon, who defended the pledging of the *assignat*.

On the fourth *jour sans-culottide* (September 20), Lindet read out, on behalf of the Committees, a long report on the state of the Republic which may be regarded as the program of the majority. He promised protection for the popular societies and for the members of the former revolutionary committees, in other words a political amnesty, which incidentally did not rule out prosecution for common-law offenses or violation of the law. But he repudiated, if not revolutionary repression, at least its excessive extension and above all the mass outlawing of nobles and priests: "Restore freedom to all those citizens who have been useful and can be useful." Finally, he proposed restoring to the business world the right to export under certain conditions, and, without naming Jacobins and *sans-culottes*, he categorically threatened those who dreamed of "the transfer of wealth." Lindet had been the head of the nationalized economy in Year II; without condemning it as a means of revolutionary defense, he visibly reduced its scope, and above all openly abandoned its social tendencies. There can be no doubt that he was in agreement with Carnot, and his speech revealed that those of the men of Year II who still figured on the Committees had rallied to the opinions of the majority in the Center. Later on, Lindet maintained that at the meetings of the Committees he had gone much further in the direction of reaction: he claimed to have proposed reviewing the Law of Suspects, releasing all the "Federalists," in other words the Girondins or self-styled Girondins, and forbidding the clubs to affiliate with one another or to admit civil servants. At the tribune, in any case, he had remained much more conciliatory towards the Left. The latter kept silent, and Lindet's conclusions were unanimously approved; possibly the Mountain realized that, considering how things stood, the wisest course was not to create difficulties for the government, in order to avoid pushing it towards the Right.

But in the Sections less caution was displayed. At the meetings held on 10 Vendémiaire, Year III (October 1, 1794), the reactionaries began standing up to the terrorists again, and three meetings, including that at the Muséum which had hitherto allowed itself to be guided by the Hébertists, passed motions against the Dijon club's address. All the same, several Sections opposed the reading of Lindet's report and at least six expressed support for the Jacobins. Nothing could have been better calculated to upset the majority, for, not believing as yet in the Royalist peril, it was obsessed by the fear of an insurrection by the Sections and a new thirty-first of May. Several incidents stimulated its fear, and the Right did everything to exploit them. During the night of 23-24 Fructidor, Tallien, on returning home, was wounded by an intruder who remained unidentified; his friends attributed the attack to the "Knights of the Guillotine." On the fifth *jour sans-*

culottide, Treilhard read out the letters from Serre and Auguis, who were on mission in the Bouches-du-Rhône, on the disturbances in Marseilles. The purges and the release of the suspects had inflamed the passions of the terrorists. One of them, appointed to the post of schoolmaster at Chabeuil in the Drôme, had taken it into his head to write to the national agent in that commune that the patriots were only waiting for a signal to eliminate "by means of a second and third of September all the impure elements left in Marseilles." The letter had been forwarded to the representatives who had its author arrested on 26 Fructidor (September 12); two days later, while he was being moved to Aix, a band of terrorists released him; on the twenty-seventh, Serre and Auguis had been greeted with jeers at a meeting of the popular society. The Convention declared Reynier an outlaw and Merlin de Thionville took the opportunity to inveigh once more against the Jacobin Club, "that den of brigands." But that was not the end of the affair. Jeanbon had promptly sent reinforcements to Marseilles and, in return, summoned a battalion from the Corrèze which was garrisoned at Avignon, where it had gone over to the reaction; in the absence of Goupilleau, who was then at Carpentras, this battalion refused to obey the summons and started fighting the workers who supported the revlutionary committee and the club. Hurrying back to Avignon, Goupilleau sent the soldiers away but also disarmed the patriots, reorganized the committee and closed the popular society. In Marseilles, the disturbances started again on 5 Vendémiaire, Year III (September 26). Serre and Auguis were besieged in their house and roughly handled by the rioters, who demanded the release of the imprisoned patriots; that very evening the representatives appointed a military commission which ordered five executions. A considerable number of terrorists were arrested and sent to Aix and to Paris; the club was purged and Carles, its president, committed suicide. The line adopted by the turncoat Montagnards who had appointed themselves the spokesmen of the Right was to depict these disturbances as the consequence of a single plot laid in Paris by the Jacobins, whose provincial societies were mere tools in their hands. On 26 Fructidor (September 12), Dumont, infuriated by the addresses praising the terrorists, had cried: "The blow comes from here: we must parry it." In Lyons, Charlier and Pocholle had followed Goupilleau's example, and from Toulon Jeanbon had advised the Committees to close the clubs. On 10 Vendémiaire (October 1), the Right succeeded for the first time in having a Jacobin address disapproved. The Committees, who also felt a certain anxiety, had, on the fourth *jour sans-culottide* (September 20), made a considerable concession to the Right, with a decree expelling from Paris all those who had not been living there on 1 Messidor, and consequently all the departmental delegates.

In these circumstances, the sectional agitation of 10 Vendémiaire produced a violent reaction. On the twelfth (October 3), the counterrevolutionaries of the Lepeletier Section complained that two days earlier the terrorists had succeeded in dominating their meeting, and they obtained the arrest of the victualer Chrétien, a former juryman in the revolutionary court, as well as of Clémence and Marchand, leading Jacobins whom the Committee of General Security had recently released. Then, after the William Tell Section had urged the Convention to "reassure Paris," Legendre took the opportunity to renew Lecointre's attack on Collot, Billaud and Barère: "I declare this to the Convention: I regard them as conspirators." Reacting vigorously, the accused asserted that the members of the Committee of Year II were jointly responsible, having always deliberated together. Carnot, Lindet and Prieur de la Côte-d'Or, who still formed part of the government, courageously testified that they were telling the truth: "I was present at all the Committee's deliberations; it is untrue that I was banished to my office, as has been stated," said Carnot, who, in Prairial, would maintain the contrary. "All the Committee's decisions were taken unanimously, apart from the police decrees which were signed only by Robespierre, Saint-Just and Couthon." (This last statement, incidentally, was false). The discussion took on an even wider scope when Cambon, attacked in his turn for not having opposed the thrity-first of May as a member of the first Committee of Public Safety, revealed the divisions which had existed in the Committee on the eve of that day, invoked the protest which he and Bréard had recorded in a secret register, and placed the responsibility on Danton. Judging by this, it was fairly certain that if the reaction triumphed, the thirty-first of May would not fail to be repudiated.

The majority had not yet reached that stage; it was still reluctant to begin its own trial, and Thibaudeau has left us a record of its hesitations. On Legendre's accusation, it went back to its agenda and left the question of the thirty-first of May in abeyance. All the same, on 15 Vendémiaire (October 6), it finally succeeded in establishing itself in the government; by the normal process of change, Carnot, Lindet and Prieur de la Côte-d'Or left the Committee of Public Safety, while Amar, Dubarran and Bernard de

Saintes left the Committee of General Security; the last men of Year II had gone. Neither the Committees nor the majority, however, abandoned their middle-of-the-road policy. Carnot and Lindet continued, in fact, to co-operate with the government. On 12 Vendémiaire, when Fréron called for an inquiry into the government officials' attitude to the ninth of Thermidor and an inspection of the registers of the revolutionary committees, Bourdon demanded that the prerogatives of the Committee of General Security should be respected. Nor did the majority take any radical measures with regard to the popular societies. On 25 Vendémiaire (October 16) it confined itself to forbidding them to affiliate or to organize collective petitions, and to taking steps to insure that lists of their members should be published. It would appear that it had come to an agreement on this issue with the Left, for the *rapporteur* of the decree was Delmas, who had presided over the Club in Fructidor; Billaud and Collot remained silent. Once again, therefore, the Montagnard Deputies revealed themselves ready to cut their losses; once again, the Jacobins complained of their inertia, though they made no attempt to resist.

Could they have done so, and were the Convention's fears justified? In his *Souvenirs thermidoriens*, Duval maintains that, but for the *jeunesse dorée*, the Assembly would inevitably have succumbed "under the blows of the Jacobins and the two horrible *faubourgs* . . . in other words at least three-quarters of the population, the aforementioned three-quarters consisting of pickpockets and thieves." It would follow that not only the laborers and workers, but also the artisans and shopkeepers, were still on the side of the Jacobins—an interesting admission to note. But apart from the fact that Duval never missed an opportunity to exaggerate the merits of the young bourgeoisie to which he had the honor to belong, it is clear that the Jacobins no longer had the means to organize a *journée*, nor would they ever have again.

It should be noted first of all that, as popular agitators, they were not alone and never had been; it might even be said that, among the *sans-culottes*, the *enragés* and Hébertists had exerted far greater influence because, being advocates of direct government, they persistently attacked the deputies, and because from the social point of view they were far bolder. Having been persecuted by the revolutionary government, they turned against it after the ninth of Thermidor, in contrast to the Jacobins, who called for its continuation; they called for the free election of local administrative bodies, and, in order to give ample play to their propaganda, joined with Fréron in defending freedom of the press. As early as 7 Fructidor (August 24), Chasles came forward as their spokesman in the Convention, when he proposed elections for the new revolutionary committees. Soon Legray, whom the ninth of Thermidor had rescued from prison, turned the Museum Section into a stronghold of the party and, on 10 Fructidor, persuaded it to demand in addition the election of a municipal council. Passed on to the other Sections, this address divided the Republicans of the Left: it was adopted, at least, by the Montreuil Section, whereas fourteen other Sections rejected it, and did so under the influence of the Jacobins, for on 22 Fructidor the Mutius Scaevola Section condemned it as "a Moderantist system." The Hébertists also turned their attention to the popular societies, which had revived to some extent after the fall of Robespierre;

35

the one that met in the hall of the electoral body, that is to say at the bishopric where the *journée* of the thirty-first of May had been organized, fell under their influence; on 20 Fructidor (September 6) it voted a petition at the instigation of Varlet, who had been one of the leaders of the *enragés*, and of the engraver Bodson. Two days later a decree restored the hall to the Hôtel-Dieu, and soon afterwards Varlet and Bodson were arrested; but Legray joined the club to the Museum Section and on 10 Vendémiaire (October 1) club and Section together drafted a new address demanding an elected municipal council. Finally Babeuf came on the scene. Prosecuted during the Terror for having, as administrator of the district of Montdidier, signed a record of allocations of national property which turned out to be fraudulent, imprisoned, and then released not long before the ninth of Thermidor, he laid the blame for all his misfortunes on Robespierre and fought fanatically against the revolutionary government and the terrorists. On 17 Fructidor (September 3) was published the first issue of his *Journal de la liberté de la presse*, in which he supported Fréron; on 14 Vendémiaire (October 5) this became the famous *Tribun du peuple*. Yet it is impossible to doubt the sincerity of these agitators, or to state for certain that there was deliberate collusion with the leaders of the reaction. Babeuf was penniless, and it was the printer Guffroy who published his paper: the turncoat terrorist used him in order to attack their common enemies, the Jacobins. But soon the *Tribun du peuple* would break with Fréron, and in Brumaire Guffroy would withdraw his support from Babeuf, who would be imprisoned. As for Legray, if one passage in the Museum address of 10 Vendémiaire called for free trade, something to which

both *enragés* and Hébertists had always been radically opposed, that is not enough to prove that he was in collusion
with the reaction: the petition was also directed against
requisitioning, which was blamed for causing the disap-
pearance of provisions from the markets and for bringing
about the general shortage of food. Besides, Babeuf immediately protested. In point of fact, the Hébertists turned,
as did Babeuf himself, against the leaders of the reaction
when they understood their maneuver. In Brumaire, when
the reaction won the day, they in their turn fell victims to
it. Legray was arrested; the Museum Section, having changed
hands, served notice on the club.

There is no reason, moreover, to attribute a very great
influence to these men. Their diversion helped to bewilder
the *sans-culottes*; but they were bewildered already, having
seen the Montagnards outlawing one another since the
previous winter and the Committees of Year II singling out
for attack the *enragés* and the Hébertists, for whom the
common people had shown a special predilection. The Jacobins no longer had any orators or journalists capable of
rousing the mob to enthusiasm, and in order to stir the
mob it was not enough to call for the imprisonment of the
suspects. To begin with, the mob no longer had the impression, as in 1793, that the Revolution was in mortal
danger; the Republican armies were victorious and the
Vendée was in its death throes. Then too, it had supported
the Montagnards only on condition that the *maximum* be
put into effect; but the *maximum* was now being abandoned,
and it was in vain that the *sans-culottes* complained that it
had been violated. The Jacobins scarcely ever mentioned it,
either in the Convention or at their club, and seemed resigned to its failure. Moreover, it had divided the *sans-*

culottes themselves, who were not a class party and included, as well as the proletariat, artisans and shopkeepers
who were eager to see the peasants' provisions taxed and
requisitioned, but most unwilling to suffer the same fate;
the workers themselves had opposed the fixing of wages,
and not without reason, for since the Committee of Public
Safety had reserved the entire benefit of the *maximum* for
the State, the civilian population had scarcely profited from
it except as regards the price of bread. For want of time
and money, the Montagnards had been unable to obtain
any great advantages for the poor, especially the poor in
the towns, by their social policy; the decrees of Ventôse had
not been applied and the proposals put forward by Duquesnoy and Fayau concerned only the peasants; the Treasury being empty, the laws on education and public assistance remained more or less a dead letter. Disillusionment
was profound, and at the approach of winter, the scarcity
and rising cost of food constituted the sole preoccupation of
most people. However, poverty was not yet so widespread
as to stir the common people to action: the cold weather
had not yet arrived; the Committee of Public Safety was
provisioning Paris to the best of its ability; the *maximum*
was still in operation and the *assignat* had not yet lost all
its value; the armaments workshops had not closed down
either, so that unemployment was not too serious. Finally,
it should not be forgotten that since 1793 a considerable
number of *sans-culottes* had left Paris for the army, and
that after the ninth of Thermidor a good many popular
agitators had been guillotined or imprisoned; thus the personnel of the *journées* had been considerably reduced.

Besides, even supposing that the common people had
been ready to rise, the Jacobins no longer possessed the

same means of mobilizing them as on the tenth of August or the thirty-first of May. As democrats, they had tried to reconcile their dictatorship with universal suffrage by imposing their views on the people's representatives by intermittent demonstrations or by the implicit threat of repeating them. In order to organize these demonstrations, they had not thought of enrolling the *sans-culottes* in the cadres of a party, and had contented themselves with the cadres which democracy offered them, taking control of the Sections, the National Guard and finally the Commune. Once in power, they had identified themselves with the State, to the extent of reducing the *sans-culottes* themselves to passive obedience, executing or imprisoning the *enragés* and the Hébertists who tried to turn the same pressure methods against them, and depriving the people of the right to choose its administrators. The Committee of Year II had itself appointed the Robespierrist Commune and the general staff of the National Guard; for the committees of the Sections themselves, it had only allowed candidates to be presented to it. In losing control of the Government after the ninth of Thermidor, the Jacobins had therefore lost everything, for the popular societies—which moreover had never included more than a small number of *sans-culottes*—were in no way organized to resort to force.

The Convention had only to continue along the same lines as the Committee of Public Safety of Year II to complete the disorganization of the Jacobin insurrectionary cadres. It had taken good care not to reconstitute the Commune. Since the ninth of Thermidor, the Committees had been administering the capital themselves: at first they confined themselves to nominating a few police officials; on 14 Fructidor (August 31), the Convention created two municipal commissions, one for the police, the other for taxation, while one official for each section was delegated to the Registrar General's office; as for the new revolutionary committees, they were chosen by the Committee of General Security; finally, since 8 Germinal (that is, long before the ninth of Thermidor), the Committee of Public Safety had been in charge of provisioning. Thus Paris had lost the right to administer itself, a right which indeed it has never recovered. As for the Sections, on 4 Fructidor (August 21), the indemnity of 40 sols granted to those citizens who attended their meetings was suppressed, on the thoroughly justified assumption that as a result fewer *sans-culottes* would attend; moreover these meetings were confined to the tenth day of each decade. As early as 19 Thermidor (August 6), the command of the National Guard had been suppressed as well as the permanent general staff, whose duties were henceforth assigned in rotation to the commanders of the Sections. Finally, on 1 Fructidor (August 18), the Committee of Public Safety had canceled its newspaper subscriptions, a measure which was aimed exclusively at the Jacobin papers and which damaged them severely.

In 1792 and 1793, the *journées* had triumphed, thanks to the connivance of the municipal authorities, and of an executive which was either disarmed or sympathetic. Already in Ventôse, Year II, the Hébertists had on the contrary failed in the face of the Committee of Public Safety's determined attitude. The situation had now altered to such an extent that it was against the Jacobins that the new *journées* were organized, under the leadership of the Thermidorians of the Right and with the resigned tolerance of the majority.

CHAPTER FOUR

The Outlawing of
the Jacobins

The method employed by the reaction to fight the Jacobins was to unite their enemies: Republican bourgeois,
Constitutional Monarchists and supporters of the *ancien
régime*. Up to 1793, they had fought against one another
as much as against the *sans-culottes*, and it was this which
had enabled the latter to seize power; the lesson had been
learned. Not that they were now agreed on what form of
government to adopt; that was impossible. But having
suffered together from the Terror, and being threatened by
both political and social democracy, they had only one idea

41

for the moment: to take their revenge on the Jacobins and to reduce the *sans-culottes* to a state of submission.

They accepted as their leaders the turncoat terrorists Tallien, Fréron and Merlin de Thionville, who had a great many things to expiate and who wanted to start a new career. A group of publicists whose personal interest demanded a return to freedom of the press gave valuable help; they included Dussaulx of the *Correspondence politique*; the Bertin brothers, who owned the *Débats*; Michel, of the *Quotidienne*; Isidore Langlois, of the *Messager du soir*; Richer de Sérizy of the *Accusateur public*; Martainville and Fiévée. The most notable of these men was probably Charles de Lacretelle or Lacretelle the Younger, who has left us some delightful *Souvenirs*, and who ran the *Républicain français* from Pluviôse, Year III, onwards. Most of these men later graced the Royalist press up to and into the period of the Restoration, but as yet they were careful to conceal their true opinions—with the exception of Sérizy, who soon started playing the part of *enfant terrible*. They worked in close collaboration, meeting to dine together and decide on the themes of their campaigns. They were hand in glove with Fréron, who was a friend of Dussaulx and who himself, on 25 Fructidor (September 11), revived his *Orateur du peuple*. For his part, Tallien, with Méhée as his secretary, created the *Ami du Citoyen* on 1 Brumaire (October 22). It was alleged that they even had accomplices among their adversaries: Ange Pitou, who contributed to Chasles's *Ami du peuple* and to the *Annales patriotiques*, was accused by Babeuf of being an *agent provocateur*. They promptly took over the field, for the Jacobins had been deprived of their government subsidies and, as Duhem remarked, did not have Thérèse Cabarrus' riches at their disposal. From Fructidor onwards, the gazettes were supplemented by countless pamphlets. In this Thermidorian press, principles occupied an unimportant place: the method used was to insult the Jacobins and to intimidate their leaders by means of continuous denunciations. They were called "drinkers of blood," "sectarians," "dominators," "thieves" who had robbed the rich for their own profit, and "anarchists" who had given lowly citizens posts which belonged by right to "decent people," in other words to the notables. The attacks on Cambon, the "executioner of the rentiers" and the "Robespierre of landed property," and on Lindet, the director of the nationalized economy hateful to all French businessmen, underlined the social character of the movement, as did the enthusiastic support of society people, whose salons were opening their doors again, and that of the singers, actors, dancers, songwriters and musicians whom the spartan regime of Year II had deprived of a remunerative public. In the Convention, the Montagnards were not alone in protesting at the blackmail and calumny practiced by this press, and on several occasions there was talk of a repressive law—but this never came to anything.

Without the slightest doubt, it was the excesses and abuses of certain terrorists that helped the leaders of the reaction most of all. Their chief targets were the revolutionary committees; the proceedings for embezzlement and falsification of records brought against the committee of the Bonnet Rouge Section, six members of which were sentenced to imprisonment on 7 Brumaire, Year II (October 28, 1794), encouraged their campaign, and on 8 Floréal (April 27, 1795) the dramatist Ducancel attained a tremendous success with a play entitled *L'intérieur des com-*

ités révolutionnaires, which put the finishing touches to the Thermidorian legend of the terrorist institution. But the biggest windfall was the trial of the 132 citizens of Nantes, which gave rise to two further trials that completed the defeat of the Jacobins. These citizens of Nantes had been arrested pell-mell after the defeat of Entrammes, when there was a rumor of a plot to hand the city over to the Vendée rebels; they had been sent before the revolutionary court and this journey, in the middle of winter and in appalling conditions aggravated at will by a hostile escort, had proved fatal to a good many of them. In Paris they had found defenders, notably Réal, and had been lucky enough not to be brought to trial before the ninth of Thermidor; on the fifth of that month, moreover, the representative Bô had had the committee which had charged them arrested and likewise sent to Paris. The trial of the ninety-four survivors began on 22 Fructidor (September 8). The leader of the accused, Phélippes *alias* Tronjolly, former president of the criminal court of Loire-Inférieure, had the members of the committee subpoenaed as witnesses and accused them of the drownings and executions without trial which had occurred; they admitted the facts and threw the responsibility on Carrier. Tronjolly and his companions were triumphantly acquitted on the twenty-ninth.

The press immediately seized on the facts revealed in court; on 29 Fructidor there appeared the pamphlet *Les jacobins démasqués*, on 7 Vendémiaire (September 28) Méhée's leaflet on the drownings, and on the twenty-sixth (October 17) Martinville's pamphlet *Les jacobins hors la loi*, while Babeuf also published one entitled *Du système de dépopulation ou la vie et les crimes de Carrier*.

In the Convention, on 8 Vendémiaire, the "infernal columns" were indicted, and Duroy, a Montagnard, obtained a decree ordering the arrest of General Turreau and two of their other commanders. From then on, Carrier hardly dared appear again at the Asssembly. Apparently neither the Convention nor the Committees were eager to pursue the matter, for a fresh incident was required to force them to do so. On 22 Vendémiaire (October 13), the Convention was confronted with the documents which stated that Sergeant-Major Lefèvre had had forty-one Vendée prisoners, nearly all women and children, put on board ship at Bourgneuf, on 5 Ventôse, Year II, with orders for the captain to throw them into the sea—orders which were duly carried out. A decree was passed ordering him to be arrested, together with those who had obeyed his instructions. Dumont took advantage of the Assembly's emotion to express surprise that nearly a month had passed without the Nantes committee being brought to trial for the actions which it had admitted, and the Convention agreed without discussion to send the case before the revolutionary court. A second trial accordingly opened at which Carrier, called as a witness, promptly took on the appearance of an accused man. Consequently, on 29 Vendémiaire, Dumont proposed submitting his case to the Committees; this was tantamount to giving them back the right to indict deputies, and Tallien protested. It was agreed that the procedure should be regulated by a law which was passed on 8 Brumaire (October 29). Any charge made against a representative of the people had to be referred to the Committees, but they would confine themselves to hearing the accused and forming an opinion without giving their reasons; if they were in favor of prosecution, a commission of twenty-one members would carry out an inquiry, and on the basis of its report the Convention would authorize or refuse a trial after hearing the deputy concerned in public session. That very evening, lots were drawn for the commission to investigate the case of Carrier.

As this commission did not present its report until 21 Brumaire (November 11), the agitation had plenty of time to grow. The Jacobins were in a difficult position. Robespierre had recalled Carrier and had intended to prosecute him in order to separate his cause from that of the Revolution, while Carrier had tried to cover himself by helping to bring about Robespierre's downfall; the result was that his trial, as was pointed out to the Jacobins, was serving as a weapon against "all the men of the Revolution." They did not dare to defend him openly and confined themselves to protesting at the intrigues against the accused. The charge against the Nantes committee was in fact being printed, posted, and distributed, and the police received countless notifications that there would be an insurrection if Carrier was acquitted by his colleagues or escaped his judges. However, by dint of repeating—rightly, as it happened—that they were the real targets, certain Jacobins lost their tempers and started uttering threats in their turn. It was Billaud, doubtless exasperated at being criticized for his reserve, who on 13 Brumaire made the most rash pronouncement:

> The lion is not dead when it dozes, and on its awakening it exterminates all its enemies. The trench is open; the patriots are going to bestir themselves again and urge the people to awaken.

This was more than enough for the Jacobin plot to save Carrier to become an article of faith for the reaction; it was an excellent excuse for extorting the indictment from the Convention and for simultaneously launching an attack on the hated club.

The leaders of the reaction had been preparing for this for a long time. Since 1793 the *sans-culottes* had been masters of the street, and in spite of the divisions in their ranks they were still a force to be reckoned with there. The Thermidorian press frequently denounced the "swashbucklers" and the "revolutionaries with big sticks" who attacked its hawkers, dominated the section meetings, and, with their womenfolk, filled the galleries of the Convention. However, immediately after the ninth of Thermidor, their adversaries had been able to gauge their own strength by gathering outside the gates of the prisons and by besieging the Committee of General Security to demand the release of the suspects. When the final break occurred between the Jacobins and the turncoat terrorists, the latter, who knew rioting technique from experience, undertook to organize a shock force to oppose their enemies, and they recruited it from the middle-class youth. This was not entirely an innovation, since at the end of 1792 it had already demonstrated in groups against the Montagnards; this time it had much greater success. According to Duval, who was then a notary's clerk, all the clerks attached to the courts of justice and most of the shop assistants and bank clerks answered the call. These young men undoubtedly shared the opinions of their class; they also derived a pleasure from demonstrating which befitted their age. But often they had a more direct interest in what they were doing: many of them were absentees, for whom the downfall of the revolutionary government meant security. Carrier, in fact, had denounced them as early as 18 Fructidor

(September 4), and on the twenty-fifth a police report stated that in a raid on the boulevards five of the thirty people arrested had been found to be absentees. What is more, Duval prided himself on the fact.

> They pretended not to notice [he wrote of his leaders] that we were all or nearly all absentee conscripts; they considered that we would be more useful to the commonweal in the streets of Paris than in the Army of the Sambre and Meuse, the Rhine and Moselle or the East Pyrenees, and anyone who had proposed sending us to patrol the frontiers would have had a poor reception, believe me.

It was in vain that the matter was raised several times in the Convention. On 14 Ventôse (March 4, 1795) an article in the *Moniteur* would praise the "young men" in terms much the same as Duval's: "While some were carrying freedom to our neighbors, the others were restoring it to France." Moreover, the best way of evading military service was to go into public service and thus obtain a good position at the same time. As fast as the Jacobins were expelled from the administrative services, the "young men" took their place. Once again, the Montagnards complained in vain. The same article in the *Moniteur* answered them:

> It has been suggested that the government should dismiss from all the posts to which it has been obliged to appoint them, the young men who have taken the place of the stupid, ferocious advocates of the Terror.

It may have been Fréron who had had the idea of using them; in any case they were known as "Fréron's *jeunesse dorée*." But they also regarded Tallien, Merlin de Thionville and Goupilleau de Fontenay as their leaders. The singer Elleviou, the actor Quesnel of the Théâtre français, the dancer Trenitz, the musician Souriguères, and the journalists Martainville and Langlois were their lieutenants, according to Duval. Lacretelle also claims to have been one of their leaders. The latter soon hired a number of thugs, formerly reputed to be *sans-culottes*, such as the Marquis de Saint-Huruge and the "patriot" Gonchon, who undertook the violent operations. The "young men" could be recognized by the square collars of their coats and by their long lovelocks; they were armed with bludgeons and shouted: "Down with the Jacobins! Long live the Convention!" Every evening, they would meet at the Palais Égalité, where they had their headquarters at the Café de Chartres. The leaders would come here to give their orders, which circulated from group to group. According to Duval, a system of communication had been organized which, in the event of an alert, made it possible promptly to call together associates scattered all over the city. If he is to be believed, the leaders of the reaction had gone even further:

> Acting on a proposal made by Fréron and Barras, the regenerated Committees of Public Safety and of General Security had given us some auxiliary leaders who brought us together two or three times a week, on the waterside terrace at the Tuileries, in the Luxembourg Garden, on the Champs-Élysées and in other places, and trained us so zealously that there was scarcely one of us who was not capable of using a rifle and eager to do so. . . . Some officers devoted to the Thermidorian party taught us how to drill.

In point of fact, in Prairial the *jeunesse dorée* was sent into action against the Faubourg Antoine. Its failure was pitiful; its troops could not hold their ground when the workers and artisans left their work to come down into the street *en masse*, but as the workers did not do this until the spring, the "young men" had things their own way for

49

a long time, the connivance of their employers allowing
them to leave their work to gather together at will. Even
so the tacit approval of the Convention was necessary; it
could not bring itself to refuse this approval, having very
few troops at its disposal. The National Guard, which in
any case was disorganized and practically unarmed, was
partially suspect, while the police itself does not appear to
have been very reliable: until Frimaire its reports were
hostile to the "young men," whom they described as fops,
and the attack of 19 Brumaire on the Jacobins was considered in these reports as "a plot hatched up by the aristocracy."

The surveillance committees, on the other hand, usually
played into the hands of the *jeunesse dorée*. The police
report of 20 Brumaire on Saint-Huruge is typical: "He
proves to all those citizens who do not think like him that
they are wrong by giving them a thrashing and taking
them straight away to the guardhouse, *where he locks
them up with impunity*." Obviously the Committee of
General Security and the surveillance committees which
were simply its tools regarded Fréron's gangs as their auxiliaries. Thus they were able to play their not inconsiderable
part, seizing control of the streets from the Jacobins and
forcing the hand of the hesitant majority in the Convention.

It was about the middle of Fructidor that their activity
began to be manifested. On the twelfth, the day of Lecointre's first attack on the terrorists, they demonstrated in a
threatening fashion around the Convention and on the
boulevards, shouting that they "would know how to force
the Convention to settle this business." On the second *jour
sans-culottide* (September 18), Garnier de Saintes de-

nounced them from the tribune. The next day, a deputation called to pay its respects to the wounded Tallien and
a serious clash occurred for the first time at the Palais
Égalité, between Jacobins and fops; henceforth such
clashes took place continually. In Vendémiaire, the *jeunesse dorée* also intervened in the Section meetings, which,
as of the twentieth (October 11), escaped from the control
of the *sans-culottes* and for the most part signified their
adhesion to the Convention. On the twenty-third, an embarrassed explanation from the Dijon club was read out,
and the Assembly declared that it regarded it as a retrac-
tion of the famous petition; those Sections which had
supported the petition thereupon began to repudiate it—
on the thirtieth (October 21), for example, the Fontaine
de Grenelle, which had hitherto been dominated by Raisson, a former member of the Supplies Commission and the
last president of the Jacobins. But it was the discussion of
the report on the Carrier case which provided the opportunity for decisive action.

On 15 Brumaire (November 5) uproar had broken out
in the Convention, where Billaud's rash outburst at the
Jacobin Club had been denounced. The number of defections increased, and on the sixteenth Lequinio solemnly
declared that he was leaving the Club. On the nineteenth,
Saint-Huruge led the first attack on the Club; the win-
dows were smashed with stones, the men beaten up, the
women whipped. The next day, when Duhem and Duroy
protested, Reubell retorted by proposing that the meetings
of the Club should be suspended. On the twenty-first (November 11), Romme read out the report on Carrier; it
concluded in favor of an indictment, though not without
revealing certain reservations; as Carrier had to be heard,

the issue appeared to be in doubt. In the evening, there was a tremendous crowd at the Palais Égalité, according to Duval

> because of the widespread rumor that the Jacobins were preparing to go, that very evening, to launch an armed attack on the Convention and to slit the throats of those of its members who wanted to undo the reign of the Terror.

Fréron and Tallien appeared between nine and ten. "Let us warn them while there is still time," cried the former. "Let us go and surprise the wild beast in its den. . . . Good young men, let us be on our way!" Marching along the rue Honoré, they reached the Jacobin Club and laid siege to it; the members who were holding a meeting made a sortie and the two sides came to blows. While the police were putting down the riot, the Committees passed a decree closing the Club, which the Convention ratified the next day. The more obstinate Jacobins went with Tissot, Goujon's brother-in-law, to join the popular society of the Quinze-Vingts in the Faubourg Antoine or what remained of the Cordeliers and the Club de l'Évêché, in the Salle du Muséum in the rue de Thionville (formerly the rue Dauphine), then later at a dancing school in the rue des Boucheries-Germain. But the faithful rarely turned up, and then the Committees had Tissot and Raisson arrested. At the beginning of Frimaire, the discomfiture of the Jacobins was complete; one after another, the Sections came to offer their congratulations to the Convention and inveigh against the terrorists.

Meanwhile the Assembly was hearing Carrier's declarations: he denied responsibility for the drownings and justified the firing-squad executions by the decree ordering rebels taken with weapons in their hands to be put to death

upon mere identification. He was confronted with his decrees of 27 and 29 Frimaire, Year II, which stipulated that
they be executed without trial, but he retorted that identification was not a trial and that it was for the judicial authority to which he had belonged to carry it out. Moreover
he challenged the very text of the decrees, of which the brief
contained only copies. The Convention decided to send
for the originals—which, incidentally, corresponded to the
copies—but refused to wait for them, and on 3 Frimaire
(November 23), referred Carrier to the revolutionary court.
He was sentenced to death and executed on the twenty-
sixth (December 16) along with two members of the
Nantes committee. Twenty-seven others were found guilty,
but released in consideration of the clause regarding motive,
and three were acquitted. This verdict raised a storm of
protest: on 28 Frimaire, Legendre had the twenty-seven
retained in custody in order to be indicted before the criminal court of Loire-Inférieure, and the revolutionary court
suppressed.

"The ladies of the aristocracy are beside themselves
with joy," wrote Dyzès on 23 Brumaire (November 13).
"I venture to predict that it will be short-lived." He was
completely mistaken. Apart from the fact that the resistance of the majority in the Convention was weakening
under the pressure of the *jeunesse dorée*, it was being under-
mined by the social life which was blossoming again in the
salons of Paris and whose importance has been shown by
Thibaudeau. In the front rank shone Thérèse Cabarrus—
since December 26, 1794, Madame Tallien—whom her
admirers called "Our Lady of Thermidor" aloud, and under their breaths "Our Lady of September," on account of
the part her husband was said to have played in the massa-

cres of 1792. She had left the Chaussée-d'Antin to install
herself in the Cours-la-Reine in a house built for an actress,
Mademoiselle Raucourt, known as La Chaumière; here
she lived on a grand scale and, setting the fashion for the
merveilleuses, launched the knee-length Greek dress which
left the wearer half-naked. The bankers and contractors
had quickly gathered together again all the people who
could be useful to them; Madame Récamier and Madame
Hamelin, among others, would soon be famous. Then
again, now that the storm was over, the nobles and bourgeois of the *ancien régime* who had not emigrated took
pleasure in reviving the traditions of the eighteenth century.
Thibaudeau mentions the salons of Madame de Vaisnes,
whose husband, a former State Councillor, had been a
friend of Turgot's, and of Le Hoc, a sometime head clerk
in the Navy Ministry and consul at Hamburg. There he
used to meet philosophers such as Suard and Morellet,
politicians such as Boissy d'Anglas and Siméon, officers
such as Menou and Truguet, and diplomats such as Maret
and Bourgoing. Soon Madame de Staël would hold recep-
tions which, from the political point of view, would
eclipse all the others. It was in these salons that the new
rich, who had been created by the Revolution and whose
numbers would be multiplied by speculation on the *assignat,* began to mix with the old bourgeoisie and the nobles,
to form the new bourgeoisie which reigned in the nineteenth century. It was often a very mixed society, which
forgathered with equal pleasure at the great lady's mansion
and at the houses of the actresses in vogue: La Contat, who
kept a tight hand on Legendre, and La Solier of the Opéra,
who was Merlin de Thionville's mistress. As after all great
ordeals, while some people returned to religion, others

plunged into a frenzied life of pleasure. Dancing, in particular, became all the rage. High society amused itself not only in its own homes, but in the public dance halls which were opening everywhere, at the Carmes, for example, where the priests had been massacred in September, or in the former Saint-Sulpice cemetery. The Terror had clearly unhinged a great many minds, and no eccentricity was found too shocking. The relatives of people who had been guillotined held "victims' balls" among themselves, to which the guests came with Titus haircuts, the nape of their necks shaven as if by the executioner, and a red silk thread round their throats. The men did not bare their bodies like the women, but the *incroyables* were already vying with each other in luxury and eccentricity of dress, and in weird distortions of speech.

On politics the influence of the salons was considerable. Every effort was made to attract the deputies to them, by the bankers in order to buy them, and by the reactionaries in order to win them over to the good cause.

To their faces [writes Thibaudeau], they were plied with all sorts of lures, and behind their backs they were laughed at. That was in order. But there were many of them who did not notice. . . . First of all, a few joking remarks would be made in their presence about the Revolution. How could they take offense when it was a pretty woman who was taking the liberty of making them? . . . After they had been trained to accept banter of this sort, they were imperceptibly encouraged to despise the institutions of the Republic. . . . However strong-minded one may be, it is impossible not to be influenced by the society in which one moves. One gives way at first out of politeness; false shame then prevents one from turning back, and one ends up by adopting, in spite of oneself as it were, other people's opinions. That is how the Republican party suffered a great many defections, some members made concessions and others sold themselves completely to the Royalist cause.

These remarks apply to every age, and Rousseau could have quoted them to justify his hostility to representative government. But they were especially valid at a moment when the members of the Convention, after having virtue urged upon them for such a long time, felt a burning desire for relaxation. "I would not be so bold," Thibaudeau admits, "as to deny that sometimes, without noticing, I may have been affected by this contagion, but it never robbed me of my independence." We may as well believe him. But there were not many who followed his example.

CHAPTER FIVE

The Beginning of the White Terror, the Amnesty for the Vendeans, and the Law on Public Worship

After defeating the Jacobins, the reactionaries could not be satisfied with Carrier's head; they returned to the attack on the leading terrorists. On 14 Frimaire (December 4), Dumont called for the Committees' report on Lebon; the next day, he asked for another on Maignet, who had been denounced by the inhabitants of Bédoin, a village in the Vaucluse which he had had razed to the ground. Legendre took this demand as an excuse to indict the whole Committee of Year II which had covered Maignet, while

Lecointre distributed the documents he had had printed in support of his denunciation of 12 Fructidor. Cambon, who on several occasions had attacked Tallien and "the new Antoinette," was now threatened; and Aigoin, Robespierre's friend and a commissary at the Treasury, having published a pamphlet against the Thermidorians, was dismissed together with one of his colleagues. However, the Committees continued their passive resistance: the reports that had been called for did not appear.

To force their hand, the reactionaries simultaneously launched another campaign, with a view to reinstating in the Convention those deputies who were still in prison for having protested against the second of June—the seventy-three—and also those whom the decrees of July 28 and October 3, 1793, had outlawed, because they had evaded arrest, but who had remained at liberty. If their seats were given back to them, the Right would be considerably strengthened. As early as 22 Vendémiaire (October 13), Pénières had succeeded in getting the Convention to ask the Committees for a report. However, the majority was hesitating yet again, for it was being asked to do nothing less than solemnly repudiate the *journées* of the thirty-first of May and the second of June, and implicitly admit that, in order to save itself, it had unjustly outlawed those whose reinstatement was being demanded. This was what Thuriot boldly pointed out when, on 1 Brumaire (October 22), Pénières returned to the attack. Lindet audaciously defended the thirty-first of May, and Tallien himself seemed hesitant. In the sittings which followed, the Convention confined itself to authorizing the seventy-three individually to return to their homes, where they were to remain under house arrest. But once the Jacobin Club had been closed and Carrier indicted, their friends returned to the attack, and the Committees, hoping to save Robespierre's former colleagues by making concessions to the Right, decided to give way. On the basis of a report by Merlin de Douai, the Girondin objectors were reinstated in the Convention on 18 Frimaire (December 8), as were several deputies who had supposedly resigned, such as Dulaure and Coupé de l'Oise, and Thomas Paine, who had been excluded as a foreigner. Altogether, seventy-eight deputies returned to the Convention, including moderates such as Daunou, but also some ardent reactionaries—Lanjuinais, Bailleul, Vernier and Delamarre—and others who soon came to terms with the Royalists, such as Aubry and Saladin. There remained the question of the outlawed deputies. On 17 Frimaire (December 7), the decrees outlawing them had been suspended; several of them promptly presented petitions, and the committees finally resorted to a compromise: on the twenty-seventh (December 17), they were amnestied but not reinstated. The Committees had thus avoided passing any judgment on the outlawing of the Girondins. But the consequences of the return of the seventy-eight immediately became apparent: they protested violently, demanding the admission of their friends, and Reubell, who was in the chair, after declaring that the decree had been passed, had to dissolve the sitting hurriedly in the midst of an uproar.

Perhaps there had been an agreement between the government and the leaders of the Right to stop prosecuting the terrorists in exchange for these concessions, for the Montagnards and the majority had approved them without discussion. If so, Montagnards and majority were thoroughly duped, for the reactionaries refused to bury the hatchet. On 30 Frimaire (December 20), Clauzel returned to the attack on the members of the former Committee whom Lecointre had denounced, unexpectedly insisting on their connivance with the Hébertists, which enabled him to add the names of Pache and Bouchotte to the list. At least he added that they were the only culprits who remained to be punished and that all the other members of the Convention were "entitled to public gratitude and esteem." But on 6 Nivôse (December 26), he attacked the entire former Committee of Public Safety, and again called for the Committees' report as well as the reorganization of the revolutionary court. Once again the government gave way. On the seventh, Merlin de Douai pronounced in favor of indicting Collot, Billaud, Barère and Vadier; the commission of twenty-one was appointed in the evening. On the eighth, the same Merlin presented the decree on the revolutionary court whose new members were elected on the thirteenth (January 2, 1795). The same day, a dramatic incident showed how far Carnot himself, who had returned to the Committee of Public Safety on 15 Brumaire, had fallen into disfavor. In announcing the recent successes of the Republican armies, he made this remark: "In view of these events, you must forgive the English if they regard our volunteers as dreadful terrorists." There was a furious uproar. "That's a remark worthy of Barère," cried Tallien. "It's a positive carmagnole," added others, while Bentabole described it as "an appalling insult to our soldiers." Carnot made an *amende honorable*: "The phrases of which Bentabole complains could, I admit, present a certain danger"; and he submitted in advance to the threat of proscription: "I recognize that governments must answer for all their actions and for the principles which have motivated them."

However the Committees had not given way all along the line: they had exonerated David, who was released from prison, as well as Voulland and Amar. It was probably in agreement with them that several attempts were made to put an end to all the prosecutions. On 18 Frimaire (December 8, 1794), Cambacérès had proposed a general political amnesty, excepting only the Royalists; Boudin did the same on 26 Nivôse (January 15, 1795). Champigny-Aubin tried to save at least the lives of Barère and his fellow accused by demanding the abolition of the death penalty on 1 Pluviôse (January 20). It was in vain: "We want no amnesty," declared Lecointre. All the same, the Committees were bold enough to clear Maignet, on 17 Nivôse (January 6), and they adjourned indefinitely the report on Lebon; the commission of twenty-one did not hurry either, for two months went by before it pronounced judgment. From time to time the Montagnards counterattacked. On 11 Nivôse (December 31, 1794), Duhem read out some long extracts from a pamphlet by a Feuillant called Lacroix, whom he succeeded in having charged with incitement to the restoration of the monarchy. Again, when Courtois' report on Robespierre's papers was printed, the Left raised a storm of protest on 29 Pluviôse (February 17), denouncing its deliberate omissions; Dumont and Legendre, who had addressed obsequious letters to the "Tyrant," complained of persecution. The *sans-culottes* had not disappeared from the streets or the Sections, and they were still demonstrating in the galleries. The majority, incidentally, took care to prove the purity of its Republican opinions by decreeing a holiday to commemorate "the rightful punishment of the last King of the French."

The reactionaries therefore continued to denounce a Jacobin plot, hatched this time to save the terrorists on the Committee. "You would be easy in your minds," declared Merlin de Thionville on 24 Nivôse (January 13, 1795), "if you did not have three great culprits to try." They did everything to exploit opportune incidents. On the twenty-seventh, a volunteer in the Eighth Paris Battalion who had reported a worker's remarks to the police was mortally wounded by the accused man, who was guillotined a few days later without anyone explaining what the soldier was doing in the capital. On 7 Pluviôse (January 26), the reactionaries brought up the new disturbances in Marseilles, where a riot had obliged the representatives Escudier and Esprit to bring the criminal court and the departmental administration back from Aix, as well as to release several of the people involved in the Vendémiaire affair; their orders were revoked and they were recalled, as was Saliceti, to be replaced by Chambon, Mariette and Cadroy, who would favor the White Terror. The Right countered the holiday of the twenty-first of January by getting another decreed for the anniversary of the ninth of Thermidor. The denunciations continued: Foussedoire, Babeuf, and Fouché, who admitted his connections with the latter, were attacked from the tribune. On 9 Pluviôse (January 28), Duhem, the most stubborn of the adversaries of the Right, was sent to the Abbaye. The petitions from the Sections became more and more violent. The Unity Section declared on 13 Nivôse (January 2) that it had denounced the Septembrists to the Committee of General Security; on 11 Pluviôse (January 30), the Temple Section attacked its

former revolutionary committee—"Strike down those tigers!"—while Lepeletier inveighed against all the terrorists.
"Let them all die," the Social Contract Section had said before, "or rather let them be deported." But, for the second
time, it was to the gangs of the *jeunesse dorée* that the
Right resorted to break the resistance of the moderates.

As of at least 25 Nivôse (January 14, 1795), their ex-
ploits increased in number. They now began attacking the
Jacobin cafés, but the "young men" also made an unexpected and curious attempt to win over the *sans-culottes* of
the suburbs; they sent them delegations to invite them to
fraternize and brought some of them over to their side by
giving them a dinner at Février's at the Palais Égalité. On
the twenty-ninth, the *Messager du soir* announced their
decision to clean up the galleries of the Convention and to
burn publicly, on 2 Pluviôse, a dummy representing a blood-
stained Jacobin, which in fact they did. On 30 Nivôse (January 19), Gaveaux, an artiste at the Théâtre Feydeau, had
sung at the William Tell Section his song, *Le Réveil du
peuple contre les terroristes*, for which Souriguères had
composed the music and which became, for some months,
the reactionaries' marching song—while the *Marseillaise*,
described as the song of the "drinkers of blood," was
banned. Then began the war of the theaters; during the first
days of Pluviôse, the reactionaries forced the Jacobin actors
—Fusil at the Théâtre de la République, Trial at the Opéra
—to make honorable amends; at every performance they
called for *Le Réveil du peuple*, a request which generally
started a general fight, the Jacobin pit replying with jeers
and revolutionary songs. Finally, on 12 Pluviôse (January
31), at Martainville's instigation, they started a hunt for
busts of Marat, beginning at the Salle Feydeau. The Com-

mittees had the busts replaced. On the fourteenth, they were knocked over again, and this time the disorder spread to the streets and the cafés. In the rue Montmartre, a bust was thrown into the gutter. As the *sans-culottes* protested, the fighting became more or less general. The Committees soon yielded, and on the twentieth (February 8), Dumont put a proposal, which was carried without opposition, that interment in the Panthéon and other similar honors should no longer be bestowed until ten years after the death of the person concerned. This measure was retroactively effective: on the twenty-first, the busts of the martyrs of the Revolution, and David's two pictures showing the death of Marat and that of Lepeletier, were removed from the hall of the Convention while the *jeunesse dorée*, massed in the galleries, sang *Le Réveil du peuple*. Not only Marat, but also Bara, Viala and General Dampierre, who had given their lives for their country, were taken out of the Panthéon. At the same time, the Club Lazovski in the Faubourg Marceau was closed, as was the Club des Quinze-Vingts in the Faubourg Antoine. An order was once again given for Babeuf to be arrested, and he evaded imprisonment only for a short time. As a sign of the times, the *Moniteur* had abandoned its usual neutrality for the first time on the seventeenth, publishing a violent article against Marat and reproducing the famous circular of September, 1792. In the Convention, the fear of a Jacobin rising had once again overcome all hesitation. On the twentieth, Mathieu had attacked, not the *jeunesse dorée*, but "the more dangerous activities" of the *sans-culottes* who were standing up to it. "A plot was on the point of being carried out," Bailleul declared on 29 Pluviôse (February 17), "whose object was nothing less than the killing of a hundred members of this assembly and the restoration of the scaffolds which you have destroyed."

The *jeunesse dorée* now considered itself so powerful that by urging it to keep calm, Fréron abruptly lost his popularity: it publicly burnt his paper and it was in vain that he tried to rehabilitate himself by attacking the 1793 Constitution. On 2 Ventôse (February 20), the Royalist Lacroix was acquitted by the revolutionary court, and the Sections obtained a decree abolishing the symbolic "mountains" which had been set up almost everywhere. They submitted more and more petitions demanding the punishment of the four accused deputies, the recall of the outlawed Girondins, the disarming of the terrorists and their exclusion from public offices; on 14 Ventôse (March 4), the Montreuil Section explicitly repudiated the thirty-first of May, which a pamphlet by Isnard had just denounced. Massacres had begun at Lyons and in the southeast, and soon the call for killing spread to Paris. On 4 Ventôse, Rovère, attributing to the terrorists a murder committed in the Comtat, had exclaimed: "If you do not punish these men, there is not a single Frenchman who is not entitled to slit their throats." The next day, an address from the popular society of Marseilles was read out:

> Representatives, the people of Marseilles have risen against the thieves, cutthroats and despots. . . . Order their arrest; order it for their own safety, for it is only a step from resistance to attack, and a step which is easily taken when bloody crimes have been committed and indignation is at its height.

In the past, the terrorists had represented exceptional repressive measures as a means of preventing a massacre of the suspects: the Committees reasoned in the same way, especially since, with the worsening of the economic crisis, hardship was bringing the common people back to Jacobinism. On 10 Ventôse (February 28), Boissy d'Anglas reported that crowds were gathering again outside bakers' shops. "It isn't the young men that are to be seen there," declared Bourdon; "it's Robespierre's rabble, the men he used to hire."

As early as the fifth (February 23), Merlin de Douai had obtained a decision that throughout the Republic the civil and military officials who had been dismissed or suspended since the ninth of Thermidor should retire to the communes where they had been living before that date, and remain there under the supervision of the municipal authorities, under the pretext that it was they who were fostering the disturbances. This was the way in which the refractory priests had been removed from their residences in the past. Here it was a Law of Suspects in reverse, and in the south of France, at least, it marked them out for massacre. Immediately afterwards, Merlin de Thionville protested at the slowness of the commission of twenty-one; "Did Brutus delay so long before assassinating Caesar? Why should the French people whom you represent have any need of a court?" But the majority still wanted to act legally. On 12 Ventôse (March 2), Saladin finally presented the report, which concluded in favor of the indictment of Barère, Billaud, Collot and Vadier. This was agreed without discussion after Legendre had obtained a decree ordering their immediate arrest. Vadier, however, remained impossible to find. On the eighteenth, Chénier and Merlin de Douai proposed recalling the outlawed Girondins, and Sieyès, who had just come onto the Committee of Public Safety, made a long speech against the thirty-first of May. The names of La Revellière and Vitet, who

were said to have resigned, were added to those of the outlaws. There was no opposition; a few Montagnards ab-
stained, but only Goujon voted against the proposal, thus
marking himself out for future reprisals. The next day, Dumont obtained the abolition of the holiday of the thirty-
first of May. In the elections of 15 Ventôse (March 5),
Carnot had finally left the Committee of Public Safety,
which Reubell joined at the same time as Sieyès. Nothing
remained but to decide the fate of the four accused; their
hearing began on 2 Germinal (March 22). With his usual
perspicacity, Mallet du Pan, in a letter of February 18, had
summed up the evolution which, since Brumaire, had gradually been pushing the majority towards a reactionary policy:

> The Convention has once again fallen completely under
> the control of public opinion. Its procedure is to use it
> without allowing it to oppose its progress. That is the secret
> of the advantage enjoyed by the moderates and the Federal-
> ists. Thus the Assembly's strength lies outside of itself.

It lay with the gangs of the *jeunesse dorée,* in whose power
the Convention found itself just as it had formerly been in
the power of the *sans-culotte* battalions.

In similar fashion, the economic system of the revolutionary government had been upset, as will be seen later.
On 1 Ventôse (February 19), the permanent status of the
districts had been revoked and the surveillance committees
suppressed in all towns of fewer than 5,000 inhabitants;
postal censorship had been abolished in principle on 19
Frimaire (December 9, 1794) and the secret postal agency
disappeared on 1 Germinal. The releases went on, some of
them of considerable interest, such as those of Kellermann
and Miranda in Nivôse, and of Servan in Pluviôse. The

same was true of the amnesty measures: all the decrees against the Lyonese had been revoked on 14 Pluviôse (February 2); and on 30 Ventôse (March 20), the execution of all revolutionary sentences passed after the law of 22 Prairial was suspended. Already, Thibaudeau and Fréron had proposed the repeal of the Law of Suspects, and Réal had started a campaign for the abolition of the revolutionary court. The 1793 constitution was also beginning to be called in question: Fréron had belled the cat in Pluviôse, and on 11 Ventôse (March 1), he revealed the device which would make possible its destruction, by demanding the preparation of certain organic laws which were supposedly intended to complete it. On the twenty-first, Reubell expressed indignation at the current talk of returning to the 1791 Constitution, in other words to the monarchy. By revealing its secret intentions, the Right alienated some of the most ardent supporters of the reaction: Thuriot, Bentabole and Lecointre. The last two protested at the reinstatement of the outlawed Girondins. Henceforth they were called Jacobins, and Legendre insultingly compared Thuriot to Billaud-Varenne.

The progress of the reaction was greatly assisted by the return of the émigrés. Up to Nivôse, it had remained dangerous for them to come back to France. But on the eighteenth (January 7, 1795), pleas began to be made in favor of the departments which had previously been invaded, those where the enemy's retreat, especially in Alsace and the Nord, had led to a large-scale exodus of people frightened by what they had heard of the Terror, compromised by their collaboration with the enemy or—having accepted official posts under a foreign government—knowing that they were outlawed. Then, on the twentieth, Bourdon asked for a distinction to be made, among the émigrés, between the counterrevolutionaries and those who had fled from tyranny. But how was such a distinction to be made? On 22 Nivôse (January 11), Merlin de Douai proposed and had adopted an arbitrary but simple and useful expedient: peasants and workers were authorized to return before 1 Germinal. In actual fact, a great many nobles and bourgeois managed to obtain certificates. At the same time, a large number of émigrés obtained from the purged authorities documents which falsely testified to their continued residence in France. Together with the absentees and deserters, whose numbers were constantly increasing, they joined in the persecution of the Jacobins, all the more fanatically in that they believed that the reactionaries, after their victory, could not fail to restore their estates to them. Already the Convention had made an indirect concession to them by the decree of 13 Ventôse (March 3) concerning émigrés and convicted persons: their chattels had been returned to their wives and children, and the decree of March 28, 1793, which had declared null and void the rights which third parties might establish to real estate, was annulled; on various grounds the relatives of the outlaws were able to recover a large part of their sequestered property, especially in Normandy.

The Thermidorians' policy towards the Vendeans and the Chouans likewise favored a counterrevolution. After Savenay, it might have been possible to disarm part of the rebels, who were exhausted and discouraged, by means of an amnesty, although by all appearances the peace would not have lasted, since it was incompatible with the outlawing of the non-juring priests, and even less compatible with the process of de-Christianization which Robespierre

had been unable to halt. In any case, the opposite course
to conciliation had been adopted; the representatives on
mission and the generals undertook to turn the region into a
desert, after ordering the patriots to evacuate it: Turreau's
"infernal columns" seized corn and cattle, cut the hedges,
burned the villages, and, all too often, manhandled or
massacred the inhabitants. Despair, it is said, rallied 25,000
peasants to the armed bands of Charette in the Marais, of
Sapinaud in the Bocage, and of Stofflet in the Mauges. The
Committee of Public Safety ended up by attenuating these
harsh measures; Turreau was relieved of his command, and
proclamations offered a free pardon to rebels who laid down
their arms, but by the ninth of the Thermidor the result
achieved was nil. All the same, the rebel bands, separated
from one another and harried by flying columns, were
gradually diminishing in number.

Unfortunately for the Republic, it had been faced simultaneously with civil war to the north of the Loire, in Brittany, and in the wooded districts of Anjou, the Maine and
Normandy, where the Vendean invasion had spread disorder and disorganized administration. As a matter of fact,
there was never any mass rising in these regions which
could have put the nation in peril: the Chouans could form
only small bands which killed officials, purchasers of national property, and unarmed constitutional priests; robbed
public treasuries; stopped stagecoaches; hampered the provisioning of the towns; and at the very most occupied some
small unfortified town for a few days. The nucleus of the
Chouan forces had been provided by some Vendeans who
had escaped from the rout, and who had been joined by
vagabonds, absentees and deserters. The leaders were for
the most part nobles: Defay, de Geslin, de la Bourdon-

naye, Boishardy and Boisguy; but they also included a few non-juring priests and a few commoners such as Coquereau, *alias* Jean Chouan. The rebellion began in the Morbihan, in Pluviôse, Year II; its effects were particularly serious near Craon and Segré, but did not cause the Committee of Public Safety much anxiety. Defay was captured and shot, and some of the troops in the west were withdrawn to go and fight on the frontiers. However, one Royalist, Joseph de Puisaye—who had been a Constitutionalist at the beginning of the Revolution, had joined the Federalist movement in Normandy in 1793, and had thus been thrust into the ranks of the Vendeans—had realized that the Chouan rising could be turned to good account by putting it at the service of the Coalition. Between May and August, 1794, he tried to organize it, created a central council and another in the Morbihan, and divided Brittany into six commands; he then gave the reins to Dezoteux, the so-called Baron de Cormatin, and at the end of August went to England, where Pitt granted him a subsidy. He also undertook to manufacture fake *assignats* and got the Comte d'Artois to appoint him commander-in-chief of the royal Catholic army. The Thermidorian Committees were soon fully informed, for the arrest of one of Puisaye's agents enabled them to seize some revealing papers in Fructidor, at La Cour-Porrée near Dinan. But there as elsewhere, the ninth of Thermidor had done its work: the moderates, busy harrying the Jacobins, allowed the military campaign and the repression to grow sluggish. The Chouans were able to terrorize the peasants, starve the towns and cut communications.

After putting an end to the revolutionary government and the Terror, the Thermidorians saw no other way of pacifying the west than that of intensifying the policy of conciliation, and they made it a point of honor to prove that concessions restored peace. Once they had entered on this course, they went a long way. To begin with, they tried to separate the rebels from their leaders by offering a free pardon to the former while maintaining a standing order to shoot the latter. New generals were sent to the west; chief among them was Hoche, who had just been set free and who, in a proclamation issued on September 15, 1794, recalled that he too had suffered from the Terror and that it had now come to an end. The representatives interpreted their instructions in the broadest possible sense: at Fontenay they released the Vendean prisoners; Boursault extended the amnesty to the absentees, gave a sympathetic reception to Le Deist de Botidoux, a former Girondin who had gone over to the rebels, and announced in November that Boisguy was prepared to lay down his arms in return for a promise that his life would be spared. Other representatives, however, were less optimistic; the Vendeans and Chouans did not appear to have been won over, and if anything the situation was deteriorating.

The Committees were accordingly urged to go further; the offers made by the generals and the representatives, it was said, did not inspire confidence; what was necessary was for the Convention itself to brand a solemn amnesty which should include the leaders of the rebellion. On the basis of a report by Carnot, this was done on 12 Frimaire, Year III (December 2, 1794) on condition that the rebels lay down their arms within a month. It was pointed out in vain that there was nothing to prevent the émigrés from returning to take advantage of these concessions. Nonetheless, there had been no suggestion of negotiating with the Royalist leaders to offer them fresh advantages.

This third stage was reached without delay. In the Morbihan, Guezno and Guermeur restored freedom of worship, even for the non-juring clergy, on 24 Nivôse (January 13, 1795). Representatives and generals agreed to negotiations or even took the initiative. Boishardy made certain offers; de Brue and Béjarry came to Nantes and strolled about in public wearing white cockades; Cormatin went to see General Humbert and got into the Conventional Bollet's good graces by declaring that he had suspended hostilities in the Côtes-du-Nord; Bézard had recourse to the good offices of Madame Turpin de Crissé, Ruelle to those of Charette's sister. Encouraged by all this, the Chouans named their terms, without interrupting their activities: "Already four hundred patriots have been massacred," Génissieu wrote from the Sarthe on 15 Nivôse (January 4, 1795); "They are killing almost every night," Legot reported from Avranches on the twenty-sixth; "We are fighting like sheep against tigers," Boursault admitted on 4 Pluviôse (January 23); and six days later, the Chouans captured Guéméné. Nonetheless, four representatives had gone to Paris, and on 27 Nivôse (January 16), Ruelle had informed the Convention that the rebels had given a rapturous reception to the amnesty. On the twenty-third, a letter from Carnot had authorized a suspension of hostilities; Ruelle and his colleagues were authorized to enter into official negotiations, and from 24 to 29 Pluviôse (February 12-17) they held discussions with Charette and other Vendean leaders, in the presence of Cormatin, at the château of La Jaunaye, a few miles from Nantes. The agreement was ratified on the twenty-ninth by three decrees signed by the representatives. They granted an amnesty to all the rebels, returned their property to them or guaranteed an indemnity if it had been sold, even if they had emigrated, and promised financial assistance for the restoration of farm buildings. The Vendeans were dispensed from military service; they were to be enrolled as territorial guards paid by the Republic and were to keep their arms; the Royal bonds they had issued were to be redeemed up to the amount of two million livres; lastly, freedom of worship was granted, even to the non-juring clergy. Stofflet and a few others had seceded, but, practically surrounded, they treated in their turn on 13 Floréal (May 2). In the meantime negotiations had been held with the Chouans at the château of La Prévalaye, near Rennes; an agreement was concluded on the same terms on 1 Floréal (April 20). All in all, the Republic had capitulated; when the civil war began again, it was even alleged that the representatives had secretly promised the restoration of the monarchy. La Sicotière, the historian of Frotté, has shown that this allegation was unfounded.

The peace was an illusion. "We shall never surrender," Cormatin had written to Puisaye. The only result was that both Chouans and Vendeans were able to prepare in perfect security to resume hostilities; they became the undisputed masters of the west and even penetrated into fresh regions, the Calvados, the Eure and the Cotentin. In the Côtes-du-Nord, according to Palasne-Champeaux and Topsent, "as early as the end of Ventôse, the Chouans behaved like conquerors, not like culprits who had been pardoned." Bonaparte would deal with them in a different fashion. Of the Thermidorians' program he would retain the amnesty and freedom of worship, without which there could have been no agreement for a long time; but he would insist on absolute submission, would flood the region with troops, would shoot the leaders without pity, and above all would methodically disarm the peasants: from Laval, on 23 Ventôse (March 13), the Conventional Baudran had declared that this last measure was absolutely essential.

Of all these concessions, freedom of worship was the most important. As religious controversy was causing disturbances everywhere, there seemed to be no reason why the same remedy should not be adopted. It was a great innovation. Admittedly freedom of worship had been solemnly guaranteed on 16 Frimaire, Year II (December 6, 1793), and since the civil constitution of the clergy had been implicitly revoked by the decree of the second *jour sans-culottide* (September 18, 1794) which had suspended payment of the juring clergy, all Catholic priests had, in this respect, been reduced to the same condition. But many Thermidorians were as hostile to ecclesiastics, of whatever sort, as the *sans-culottes,* and therefore they had gone on treating them, until then, as they had before the ninth of Thermidor; constitutional priests had resigned in a great many places since that *journée;* those who had been arrested were released with the suspects, but several received the attentions of the police again when they tried to restore public worship. In the Haute-Garonne and the Tarn, Mallarmé had them placed under supervision in the chief town of each district, even if they had resigned, with the exception of those who had married (14 Vendémiaire, Year III [October 5, 1794]); in the Bas-Languedoc, Perrin had them arrested or sent fifty miles from their homes. Churches also continued to be closed, for example by Pelletier and Besson, on 30 Brumaire (November 20), in the

Doubs and the Haute-Saône, and by Calès in the Côte-d'Or, in Frimaire; the local authorities, even after being purged, did everything they could to prevent them from being opened again, and on 2 Nivôse (December 22), the district of Bernay forbade the celebration of the Mass. The Protestants and the Jews were not spared: the pastors of Montbéliard had to resign under the threat of arrest and the synagogue at Besançon was closed. As for the nonjuring priests, a certain number were guillotined. At the same time, observance of the tenth day of each decade was strictly enforced; the churches remained dedicated to the Supreme Being or even to Reason; the Committee of Public Instruction was asked to prepare a law on the civic religion, and in Nivôse Chénier presented some reports which, it is true, had no effect; the law of 27 Brumaire, Year III (November 17, 1794) did not forbid priests to be schoolteachers, but it maintained the exclusively secular character of education.

However, a good many French people who were loyal to the Revolution longed for the religious ceremonies of old, although the number of believers varied considerably between one region and another. The civic religion, thought up by bourgeois who had studied antiquity at school and frequented Masonic lodges, remained unintelligible to the common people, except perhaps as a symbol of that patriotic and democratic fervor of the *sans-culottes* which the Thermidorians were particularly eager to suppress. When they were told that the Terror was over, the faithful—especially the women—almost immediately made attempts to regain possession of the churches; in opposing these attempts the authorities provoked disturbances, and as the reaction became more marked, they tended to shut their

eyes to what was happening. By the end of the year, the
constitutional clergy had become active again; thus, in
Nivôse, Grégoire's vicars-general restored public worship in
Loir-et-Cher. On the first of that month (December 21),
Grégoire himself made a brave speech demanding complete
freedom of worship. Legendre replied contemptuously:

> I thought that we had gone far enough in the way of rev-
> olution not to bother our heads any more about religion.
> . . . I do not propose that we should fall in a body on the
> class of former priests. . . . But I cannot forget that it has
> always been the priests who have been the firmest pillars of
> the monarchy.

The Convention set aside Grégoire's motion in the midst
of loud applause; all the same, his speech was widely published, and many pamphlets supported him, also heaping
ridicule on the civic religion or questioning its utility. During the same period, there were reports that non-juring
priests were reappearing everywhere and celebrating the
Mass in secret: in the Nord, for example, they were known
as "the portmanteau priests," because they carried the sacred vessels around with them. The frontier departments
witnessed a great incursion of exiled priests and also of
foreign ones, especially Belgians. On 18 Nivôse (January 7,
1795), Merlin de Douai classed the exiled priests with the
émigrés, and obtained a decree calling on the authorities
to prosecute them.

But when the negotiations with the Vendeans and the
Chouans had resulted in agreement, the Committees had
to change their attitude; it was clearly impossible to refuse
to the rest of the French people what had been granted to
the rebels. On 3 Ventôse (February 21) Boissy d'Anglas
put forward a decree which was passed without discussion.

In his report he had maintained the principle of the secularity of the State—"religion has been banished from government, and it will not return"—and had shown a fine contempt for the revealed religions. "I shall not consider whether men need a religion," he had said; "if so, it has put a high price on the consolations men have received from it"; but "reason alone can triumph over error." He ended up by condemning the scandals of de-Christianization, and concluded that "religious practices are not offenses against society"; moreover, clandestine worship was more dangerous than public worship. The churches were retained for decadal observance; religious worship in public was merely authorized in buildings which the priests and the faithful would have to obtain themselves, and they were forbidden to form associations, to receive either public grants or private donations, to display any religious emblem outside, to ring bells or even to indicate by any inscription the function of the building. In addition to the constitutional clergy, those priests who, not being public servants, had not had to take the oath of November 27, 1790, but had agreed to that of August 14, 1792 (the "little oath" of allegiance to liberty and equality), were able to benefit by this decree; the non-juring priests, who were still legally liable to the death-sentence, seemed to be excluded, except in the west where they could invoke the terms of the peace agreement.

Grégoire immediately gathered together the constitutional bishops, who on 25 Ventôse (March 15) published an encyclical on the reorganization of public worship; a little later, he issued the *Annales de la religion*; clergy all over the country who had resigned applied for their certificates of priesthood, but those priests who had married were not reinstated. Some of the constitutional clergy, incidentally, began making honorable amends in order to return to the Roman obedience. Those non-juring priests who, being infirm or over sixty, had not been deported, and those Roman priests who had taken the "little oath," turned the law to great account; two of them, the Abbé Jauffret and the Abbé Sicard, also published a periodical, the *Annales religieuses, politiques et littéraires*. In point of fact, the government did not derive much benefit from its concession; the non-juring clergy went on agitating and clandestine worship prospered more than ever, while the conflicts between Roman priests and constitutional priests waxed hot again. Worse yet, the faithful could not make head or tail of this freedom of worship which forbade them admittance to their churches and the use of bells and processions; in many places they regained possession of the former with the connivance of the municipal authorities and took no notice of the law. The reactionaries, the absentees and deserters, and the returned émigrés were therefore joined by the non-juring priests and also, probably, by some of the constitutional clergy. Mallet du Pan, at least, rallied them all under his banner. "In re-creating Catholics," he wrote on March 17, "the Convention is re-creating Royalists. Whosoever goes to Mass is an enemy of the Republic. There is not a single priest who does not represent loyalty to this regime as a matter of conscience to his flock."

In the course of the winter, the excitement caused by the progress of the counterrevolution once again went beyond the intentions of the Thermidorian majority. As early as Nivôse, in Lyons and the southeast, individual killings began. Then armed bands—the famous Companies of

Jesus, of Jehu and of the Sun—were organized to hunt the terrorists, and, under this name, soon included all those who had declared their support for the Revolution, and notably the purchasers of national property. Some representatives, for fear of the Jacobins and at the same time as they were having the latter disarmed, favored the formation of these bands, as did Cadroy and Chambon in Marseilles, and Isnard at Brignoles. It has been said that the bourgeois did not join these bands, although we are told at the same time that they brought together the relatives of victims of the Terror. In fact, while they seem to have been more mixed in character than they were in Paris, they were also partly recruited from the *jeunesse dorée*. However, in the southeast at least, their role was different: they had no need to exert pressure on the representatives on mission or on the municipal authorities, for obvious reasons; their task was to carry out the mass murder of the terrorists who were arrested. The first massacre took place in Lyons on 14 Pluviôse (February 2); twelve days later in the same city, Fernex, a member of the Popular Commission of Lyons, who had just been found, was likewise killed; and after that, almost every day saw the murder of one or more Jacobins, who were known as *Mathevons*, without regard to their sex. At Nîmes, on 5 Ventôse (February 23), four prisoners were put to death. The White Terror had begun. Harried without respite for the past six months by the representatives, the Jacobins were powerless to resist, except at Toulon, where the workers at the Arsenal formed an imposing mass and could count on the support of the crews of the fleet. When Mariette arrived at Toulon to carry out a fresh purge of the municipal authorities, a riot broke out on 20 Ventôse (March 10), and seven émigrés who had been arrested on landing at Hyères, whom the authorities were accused of intending to release like many others, were massacred in their turn. The position of the Jacobins throughout the region only worsened as a result. In Marseilles, Cadroy seized the opportunity to distribute arms to the Company of the Sun. The Convention had not taken any measures so far to pacify the south of France; all the same, it must be admitted that it would not have given free rein to the White Terror if a fresh crisis had not occurred to bind the majority closely to the Right. But the time had come when the monetary crisis and the scarcity of food were to provoke popular insurrections whose defeat would complete the downfall of the Jacobins.

CHAPTER SIX

The Abolition of the Maximum *and the* Monetary *Disaster*

It is the tragic struggle between the parties which, as always, has drawn the attention of most historians to the Thermidorian period. Its importance, however, is eclipsed by the collapse of the *assignat*. By reason of its economic consequences, whose political repercussions were extremely important; by reason of the effect it had on the conduct of the war and on the revolutionary foreign policy; and by reason of the blows it struck at the social structure of the France of old, the monetary disaster was the major event of the period, and it bore heavily on the history of the Directory.

The Thermidorians brought it on by abandoning the *maximum*. The Montagnards had ended up by accepting the latter, because in order to pay for the war they would have been reduced to runaway inflation if they had not been able to halt the rise in prices. To allow that rise to continue was therefore tantamount to ruining the currency. The Thermidorians were condemned to doing this from the moment when, instead of moderating and regularizing the Terror, they stigmatized it and deprived the revolutionary government of the coercive force which sanctioned its authority. A free economy, based on the profit motive and consequently on individual selfishness, can do nothing but let things be, and is in harmony with political freedom; price limitation, on the contrary, since it reduces profit, comes up against the producer's passive resistance and is ineffective unless it is accompanied by requisitioning, which, meeting the same obstacle, soon forces the State to take over control of the national economy. From then on, dictatorship, police supervision and intimidation become indispensable to the State if it is to exact obedience. It was therefore no accident that a free economy had been advocated in the eighteenth century at the same time as civil and political freedom; for the bourgeoisie, the latter was the necessary condition of the former, in other words of capitalist expansion. Dictatorship might, at a pinch, appear to it as a temporary expedient necessary for the maintenance of its own authority, but only on condition that such dictatorship respected economic freedom. The Thermidorians proved this by restoring the latter while turning the Terror against the democrats who advocated State control, and the social character of the reaction was thus revealed for all to see. Moreover, the resistance of the Montagnards, the Jacobins and the *sans-culottes* was perfunctory because they did not oppose the principle of individual property, as understood by western civilization, but on the contrary tried to generalize it; if they limited its application, either in the name of national defense or because of the obligation incumbent on a community to guarantee each citizen the right to life, the fact remains that any *sans-culotte* who possessed some property instinctively tended to shake off the controls which he thought fit to impose on others. On 3 Nivôse, Year III (December 23, 1794), the Montagnard Taillefer would say: "The abolition of the *maximum* has been demanded on all sides; the need for it is known to every citizen."

As far as the civilian population was concerned, the general *maximum* for basic foodstuffs, laid down on September 29, 1793, had never worked properly because the Committee of Public Safety, contenting itself with providing the population with bread, had given up the idea of feeding it by means of requisitioning, except in a few instances from which Paris benefited most of all. As it was impossible to violate the *maximum* publicly without risk, the shops emptied and clandestine trade developed; all the same, as long as the Terror lasted, this trade was held in check and prices rose only slowly: people complained most of all that they could not find anything for their money. After the ninth of Thermidor, the Convention remained silent for a long time; then, on 21 Fructidor (September 7, 1794), it decided to prolong the general *maximum*, like that for grain and fodder, for the duration of Year III. At that time, the *sans-culottes*, as the petitions from the popular societies show, still imagined that the system was going to continue to be improved, and asked in particular for a tax to be imposed on cattle in order to deprive the butchers of the excuse they used in their defense. But already, as fear died down, there was a perceptible rise in prices and clandestine trade started making rapid strides. In Paris, the efforts made by the police were all in vain and not without a certain danger for themselves. "The commercial aristocracy is boldly lifting up its head," said a report on 3 Vendémiaire, Year III (September 24). Speculation in foodstuffs was already in full swing in the taverns at the Marché des Innocents, and another report noted that "the water carriers and market workers do nothing else but engage in this traffic." For their part, the workers—especially the bakers, stevedores and carters—had demanded wage rises. As early as 20 Vendémiaire (October 11), the police resigned themselves to the inevitable: "In the markets, the *maximum* is no longer observed; everything is sold by private contract." The Convention, on 17 Frimaire (December 7), would be told: "It was abolished a long time ago." Back in the middle of September, people had been saying: "We are no better off than we were in Robespierre's day, because we can't find anything and the little there is is far too expensive." Now, on the threshold of winter, the police regarded the growing murmurs of discontent as positively alarming. The Committee of Public Safety continued its distributions of food through the medium of the Parisian Sections, but they were more inadequate than ever; there was a perpetual uproar at the wood and coal docks, and many people could not obtain candles. In the provinces it was worse, for there the authorities could provide nothing but bread.

For grain and fodder, the system in force dated from the decree of September 11, 1793, which had laid down a national *maximum*, fixed, in the case of corn, at fourteen livres a quintal. It had been observed fairly well, because the decree authorized requisitioning, not only for the armies, but also for the markets. However, the former had priority: the government demanded quotas from regions which it chose at discretion, and it was to the task of obtaining these quotas that its agents devoted most of their energies. For the civilian population, on the other hand, decentralization was almost complete. It was the responsibility of the district to order requisitions for each of its markets, and it could levy them only on the villages which were in the habit of sending provisions to the market in question; in the event of shortage, it had to ask the Committee of Public Safety to levy a requisition on another district, often a long way away, and then make arrangements to obtain the corn and transport it. With the market thus theoretically supplied, supervision of the sale of corn and bread was the exclusive responsibility of the municipality; if it received very little, as was the case in the greater part of the south, the Massif Central, and the mountain regions which did not produce enough to be self-sufficient, it suppressed the market, mixed grain of all sorts together, and divided it among the citizens; to those unable to bake their own bread, it gave ration cards and supplied the bakers with a corresponding amount of grain; finally, in some cases, as at Toulouse, it set up a communal bakery. During this time, in the heavily cultivated regions, the towns left complete freedom to the markets and bakeries and ate white bread. But after the end of summer, stocks had dwindled almost everywhere and the organization of the distribution system in the cities had made noticeable progress. As for Paris, the size of its population had earned it an exceptional system: the capital was granted special requisitions, and since November 1793 the use of ration cards had been the rule.

Up to the ninth of Thermidor, the military requisitions had been carried out more or less successfully, although with considerable difficulties and delays. The towns had been provisioned only on a day-to-day basis; the bread was bad and was regarded as expensive—three sous a pound in Paris, and often five in the provinces—but supplies had not often run out, although the workers did not consider themselves satisfied with less than two pounds a day. As for the peasants, requisitioning had been the symbol of the Terror for them, and very often the only manifestation of the Terror they had known, apart from de-Christianization. If they did not comply, the bailiffs were turned loose on them, and then they were arrested as suspects, beginning with the local councilors. As soon as the Terror had stopped, they plucked up courage, started selling secretly at home, displayed growing ill will, and even refused to thresh and deliver. In Vendémiaire, the Commission of Trade and Supplies reported these disturbing symptoms in a circular to all the districts, and on the twenty-fifth (October 16) the Committee of Public Safety published a decree recommending the application of legal sanctions. But the peasants had found some defenders. On 8 Fructidor (August 25), Eschassériaux criticized the obscurity of that very decree, its arbitrary nature, and the denunciations which its application implied: "A law on food supplies should be a regulation that is easy to follow, not a penal code." Since the general *maximum* and that of wages were no longer observed, various petitions pointed out that the peasants would no longer find it worth their while to sow corn. On

19 Brumaire (November 9), a few concessions were
made to them: the failure to supply levies no longer en-
tailed the confiscation of the required quota, and the municipal councilors alone remained liable to punishment,
which in point of fact was equally illusory; the national
maximum was replaced by a district *maximum* based on
the 1790 price increased by two-thirds, the result having to
be not less than sixteen livres a quintal; on the twenty-third,
the cost of transport to the market or the warehouse was
granted in addition, if the distance exceeded five miles.
The result was that the resistance of the peasants increased;
they sensed that the Convention was abandoning the system. The towns, on the other hand, finding their supplies
dwindling, tightened up their regulations, which shows that
those regulations had been adopted only under the pressure
of circumstances.

Perhaps the Thermidorians would have left things there
if the general *maximum*, violated among private individ-
uals, had not continued to be applied to all the goods which
the State required for the maintenance of the armies, the
armament workshops and the administration; and if, again,
in order to enforce the *maximum* and encourage production, the State had not enormously increased its economic
powers to the detriment of private enterprise. It had created armament factories, notably one in Paris for the manufacture of muskets, which consisted incidentally of a large
number of scattered workshops, and had itself organized
the manufacture of saltpeter and gunpowder; next, it had
thought fit to lay its hands on the transport system, had
requisitioned the shops, the boats and barges of the inland
waterways, and the wagons and cart-horses, and had taken
over the postal service as well; it had even begun building

boats and making carts. Admittedly the greater part of the economy had nonetheless remained in the hands of private firms, which continued to operate beside the national factories and transport services, but the State had deprived them of all freedom by requisitioning them, or by giving them contracts at prices which it fixed itself. The worst of it all was that the State had taken complete control of external trade. Under the *maximum* system, the merchants could import scarcely anything; the war had increased the number of bans on sending goods out of the country, and any export gave rise to a suspicion of smuggling; the exporter was also suspected of leaving abroad the money which was due to him. The Committee of Public Safety had arrogated to itself the right of pre-emption on all imports and the control of all exports; it had forced the bankers and merchants to surrender to it their foreign bills and credits; at the same time as it had sequestered the property of the belligerents, it had also compelled its own nationals to pay into its coffers the sums which they owed the latter. Nor was that all; the war and the English blockade had aroused a strong nationalist movement in France, which shipowners and merchants had perhaps viewed favorably at first: English goods had been seized and banned, a navigation act had forbidden foreign ships to bring in goods which did not come from their own country, and an embargo had been placed on neutral ships. Once foreign trade had been brought to a standstill in this way, the Committee of Public Safety had realized that a great many products were unobtainable and that it would have to be started up again. After the outlawing of the Hébertists, it had set about this task: for one thing, it had sent a good many agents to Switzerland, Genoa, Hamburg and Copenhagen, which had not joined the Coalition; it had also suspended the navigation act and restored normal facilities to neutral shipping. Again, in Ventôse and Germinal, it had set up in the ports committees composed of merchants, and instructed them to organize the export of wines and brandies and various luxury products, on condition that they surrender to the State the foreign credits they obtained. By the ninth of Thermidor, the results achieved were far from satisfactory. Fairly large purchases had been made, but the prices had had to be haggled over and paid in kind or in currency; as exports had remained insignificant and the requisitioned bills and credits had been exhausted, the Committee began selling abroad the jewels and articles of value found in the furniture repository or in the sequestered properties; in France, it was obliged to transfer its purchases at the price laid down by the *maximum*, in other words at a loss, so that inflation, although kept within limits, continued all the same: the *assignat*, which had returned to fifty per cent of its face value in December, 1793, had fallen back to thirty-one per cent in July, 1794.

In the Thermidorian Committee of Public Safety, Lindet, who had always had supreme control over the national economy, retained his place until 15 Vendémiaire, and after that he was continually called in for consultation; moreover, he joined the Committee of Trade, Agriculture and the Arts, and became its president. The Executive Commission of Trade and Supplies and the huge bureaucracy which depended on it continued their activities, as if nothing had changed, by virtue of the momentum they had acquired. The system therefore went on functioning more or less in the same way until the end of the year. In Vendémiaire, the requisitioning was still going on: the marcs of grapes and the lees of wine were placed at the disposal of the saltpeter manufacturers; an important decree laid down regulations for the use of offal for the manufacture of candles and oil; on the twenty-second (October 13), it was decided to extend the *maximum* to cover oil seeds; admittedly a considerable number of decisions altered the system of price limitation, but many of them had already been promulgated before the ninth of Thermidor. The manufacture of military supplies, particularly of saltpeter, continued into Brumaire; the government placed contracts, accepted tenders, encouraged the activities of the national factories it had set up; the workshops which the districts had been instructed to organize to provide the troops with clothing and equipment were still in full operation; the cobblers remained under contract to supply footwear and efforts were being made to fulfill an order for a million pairs of clogs. The nationalization of transport had not been abandoned, and fresh orders were being placed for the building of wagons and boats.

But the opponents of the system were at work, and they were many and powerful. The craftsmen and the factory owners, vexed to begin with at being placed under State control and paid at the rates laid down by the *maximum*, were even more irritated at seeing the national factories taking work away from them. What is more, Carnot had never been in favor of the latter and preferred private enterprise as being more economical: on 23 Frimaire, Year III (December 13, 1794), Boissy d'Anglas would declare that a bayonet made in the Paris workshops cost fifteen livres, whereas private tenderers offered it at five livres or five livres, ten sols, and in the provinces it could be made for four livres—which did not prevent the workers in the national workshops from demanding an increase in wages. The press grossly exaggerated the number of these workers: on 30 Nivôse, the *Vedette* stated that there were 45,000 of them; in fact there were 5,300, while the private tenderers employed 1,000. Certain facts show that at an early date the government decided to make some concessions in this respect: In Fructidor, the Toulouse foundry was handed over to private enterprise, and in Frimaire, the foundry at Maubeuge; on 5 Vendémiaire (September 26), the cannon foundry at Avignon had been closed down; on 11 Brumaire (November 1), the government even authorized private contracts for the manufacture of clogs, in violation of the *maximum*. Guyton de Morveau and Prieur de la Côte-d'Or succeeded in saving the Meudon factory, which had been violently attacked by Fréron, who suspected the Jacobins of being in control there and of preparing an insurrection, but the Paris workshops ended up by going to the wall. The agitation of the workers—stirred up, so it was said, by the Jacobins—was taken as an excuse; on 28 Brumaire (November 18), the board which controlled the workshops was suppressed, and on the thirtieth, the Convention appointed a commission of inquiry. As early as the twenty-third, the Commission of Arms and Powder agreed that only repairs should be done in Paris, and that since the provincial armament factories were short of work, it would be best to transfer the current orders to them: the Parisian workers could be dispersed among the provincial factories, a proposal which reveals the political motive which finally decided the government. On 16 Frimaire (December 6), the Committee of Public Safety ordained that as of 1 Pluviôse, the Republic would cease to employ workers on a daily basis, and during the following days it ordered as many as possible to be dismissed or sent into the provinces; a decree published on the twenty-third confirmed this ordinance in spite of the demonstrations against it; on 9 Pluviôse, only 1,146 workers were left on the State's payroll, and they were on piecework. In the provinces, as fast as the municipal authorities were purged, they abandoned all interest in the revolutionary enterprises, particularly the manufacture of saltpeter.

On this point, the system had been affected only partially and indirectly; on others, it was attacked openly and undisguisedly by those who, at that time, represented capitalism: the shipowners, the merchants and the financiers. It was they who suffered from the nationalization of external trade, above all of sea trade, which at that time was still the source of the great fortunes; the requisitioning of foreign exchange had put an end to profitable speculations on the *assignat* carried out from the start by the Parisian banks, which were dominated by foreigners, Swiss, Dutch and English financiers, on a fifty-fifty basis with Baring of London, Hope of Amsterdam and Parish of Hamburg. They now had friends in the government and spokesmen in the Convention. On 28 Fructidor (September 14), a speech was made there for the first time attacking the principles of Year II. Edme Petit asked for trade to be set free again, and Bourdon spoke against the unlimited extension of requisitioning. Cambon, whose family had made its fortune in business, spoke in support, even though he was a Montagnard, protesting at the persecution of which trade had been a victim; on 14 Brumaire (November 4), he would say, even more clearly: "It is impossible for the State to be in business." The Trade Commission, he added, should satisfy the needs of the republic, "but must not engage in trade on its own account"; in other words, it should confine itself to placing orders with merchants.

On the fourth *jour sans-culottide* (September 20), fuller details were given: in his major report on the state of the Republic, Lindet, forced to make some sacrifices, admitted that commercial relations with other countries had to be re-established; and the Convention ordered a decree to be prepared which should restore freedom to export luxury products, on condition that essential foodstuffs were imported in return. This decree makes it possible to guess at the argument which had won over the Committee. It was worried about the rise in food prices, and even more about the scarcity threatened by the harvest, which had been spoiled by the disturbances and by a cold, wet summer; it was told that the only solution was to buy from abroad. Victory offered it the means of doing this: the Republican armies were about to reach Holland, and coasting towards Hamburg, the corn market of the Baltic, would become easy again as a result; in November the royal administration of Prussia would offer its corn to France through the medium of a naval engineer on a mission to Hamburg. The government lacked the means to pay for these purchases, but not the merchants, who would obtain credit and contrive to take advantage of the huge capital which they and many other Frenchmen, whether émigrés or not, had transferred abroad. The advocate of the world of trade was probably Perregaux, a Swiss banker who, in spite of his dealings with the syndicate of international speculators, had managed to get the Committee of Year II to accept his services, and who now became the gray eminence of the Thermidorian Committee. He shone in the front rank of the council which a decree of 14 Vendémiaire, Year III

(October 5, 1794), signed by Eschassériaux, instituted to advise the Trade Commission. There were nine other members, most of them provincial merchants and manufacturers. This was setting the fox to keep the geese, and Lindet's proposal was no longer adequate. On 26 Vendémiaire (October 17), the manufacturers were given back the power to import freely, and anything they bought from abroad for the needs of their workshops was exempted from requisitioning; on 6 Frimaire (November 26), the import of food and unprohibited goods became completely free. But, as Cadroy and Expert pointed out from Marseilles, the result would be nil unless goods bought from abroad were exempted from the *maximum*. At the same time, the Committee of Public Safety officially confirmed the abolition of the navigation act and made it up with the neutrals; a decree of 25 Brumaire (November 15), signed by Lindet, ordered them to be respected at sea and opened up the French ports to them again, allowing them to do business by private contract. The only exception made was for contraband of war and enemy goods as long as the other belligerents refused to admit that the neutral flag covered the cargo; even so, it was added that neutral captains should be reimbursed for the freightage of enemy goods which were a lawful prize. Cadroy and Expert concluded that it was unreasonable not to allow the French to import at the same rates as foreigners.

It is a matter for surprise that the fixing of prices, which had brought nationalization in its train, had not been attacked more frequently in the Convention. On 30 Fructidor, Year II (September 16), Villiers had declared that its abolition was the key to any reform, while hastening to add that this was unthinkable; on 14 Brumaire, Year III (November 4), the Convention had asked for a report on "the disadvantages of the *maximum*," without any result but a modification of the *maximum* for grain and fodder. Thibaudeau boasts that he was the first to dare to go to the root of the evil, on 13 Frimaire (December 3), but nothing more was heard about it until 2 Nivôse (December 22), when the decisive debate finally opened. It was as if the opponents of the *maximum*, fearing, in spite of its degeneration, popular reaction and parliamentary opposition, had thought it best, by means of secret propaganda, to obtain the Assembly's unanimous consent beforehand, so as to confront the public suddenly with a *fait accompli*.

In the open, they preferred to attack the officials of the national economy and criticize their numbers, their mistakes and their misdeeds. Control of the economy was theoretically in the hands of the Executive Commission of Trade and Supplies, but other bodies were also concerned, such as the Transport Commission and the Commission of Arms and Powder. Each of these commissions controlled numerous agencies which, in their turn, were subdivided into bureaus. There were thousands of employees and the cost was enormous; in the agency concerned with the clothing, equipment and billeting of the troops, supervision of the workshops alone involved nearly 400 clerks, most of them heads of departments; the "management" of the armament works in Paris cost, by itself, 180,000 livres. In the provinces and also abroad, a host of agents checked accounts, supervised the enforcement of requisitioning, placed contracts, guarded warehouses. In point of fact, they themselves were subject to no supervision whatever; in Paris, nothing was known about their accounts, and in spite of a formidable mass of documents it was impossible to obtain a clear idea of requirements and resources. At a time when the concentration of enterprises was barely beginning and had hardly ever passed the commercial stage, this state of affairs is hard to understand, but it lent itself to criticism, and on this point Cambon's eloquence was inexhaustible; on 8 Brumaire (October 29), he had an order sent to the Trade Commission to produce details of its purchases and requisitions, and of the use of these: it was unable to comply.

There was also much criticism of the abuse of the unlimited requisitions which filled the producers' or the merchants' warehouses with goods which were never collected; it was said too that certain agents of the government trafficked in these goods for their own profit, and there were indeed recorded instances of this. Eschassériaux devoted much of his energy to putting an end to these abuses. On 19 Vendémiaire (October 10), he called on the commissions to draw up a list of their requirements for Year III, confining themselves to absolute essentials, and, finally, he secured the passing of the decree of 19 Brumaire (November 9), which not only nullified the sanctions applied to defaulters, but also forbade unlimited requisitioning and laid down the conditions and period of future operations. In the national warehouses too, piles of goods remained unused: from Marseilles, the representatives reported in Frimaire that 8,000 hides had been immobilized for seven months. The previous month, the Convention had sent representatives to the ports with instructions to inspect the warehouses and dispose of their contents; on 12 Frimaire (December 2), it restored freedom to the trade in the prizes brought in by the privateers. The results were not exactly impressive: in Germinal, for example, there remained at Le Havre 400,000 bottles of champagne, and crates of books, window-glass, batistes, lawns, laces and silks which had been accumulated there with a view to exporting them; and in Thermidor, it was reported that there were still 1,700 barrels of wine at Bordeaux, stocked there for the same purpose.

Now politics came into the matter. The members of the commissions and their agents had been chosen in the time of Robespierre and were slow to be purged. In Brumaire, Tallien denounced them at the tribune and in his paper as terrorists, and on 23 Frimaire (December 13), the Corn Market and Lepeletier Sections attacked them at the bar: "These commissions were created simply to serve the criminal purposes of our oppressors; they are composed only of their creatures and their followers." On the thirteenth (December 3), Garnier de Saintes, after sharply criticizing their administration, had secured the appointment of a commission consisting of one delegate from each of the Convention's committees, to prepare a complete overhaul of the executive; this was the Commission of Sixteen, which, as things turned out, achieved nothing.

Nobody, moreover, had so far proposed abolishing the system created by the men of Year II to obtain directly for the State the resources in kind which it needed; all that was suggested was that the government officials should confine themselves to provisioning the armies—a suggestion which was not absolutely novel, since the Robespierrist Committee, in decentralizing control of the grain intended for the civilian population and in refusing the latter the benefit of requisitioning in respect of other essential goods, had already given a clear indication of its desire to limit its economic activity to the State's requirements. But the financiers were looking further. Up to 1793, in order to provision the armies, the government had not confined itself to abstaining from requisitioning and price-fixing: as a general rule it had not made purchases itself. For want of financial resources it had been in the habit, for centuries past, of entrusting these services to companies which maintained them on credit, but which fleeced the Treasury while their agents swindled the troops. The "commissaries" had always been the kings of finance and built up huge fortunes. It was partly in order to do without them that the revolutionary government had accepted the *maximum* and the nationalization of the economy. And it was in order to re-establish their profitable monopoly that the commissaries lured members of the Convention into their salons and preached commercial liberty and the abolition of the commissions to them.

The combined efforts of the supporters of economic freedom finally won the day. On 19 Frimaire (December 9, 1794), Giraud submitted to the Committee of Trade, Agriculture and the Arts a report which concluded in favor of the abolition of the *maximum*. The decisive defeat of the men of Year II was underlined by the retirement of Lindet, who did not sign the minutes of the meeting and abandoned the presidency, which passed to Giraud; on 11 Nivôse (December 31), Lindet even resigned from the Committee. On 3 Nivôse (December 23, 1794), the report went to the Convention, where it gave rise to a mediocre debate. Giraud was aware of the danger involved: "We must not shut our eyes to it: we may well be horrified at the temporary upheaval which may be caused by the rapid rise in prices which will occur at first." Lecointre, who asked that a *maximum* be retained for grain, showed that he saw disturbances ahead. Pelet above all, without being a supporter of fixed prices, argued strongly against the hurried abolition of the *maximum*, asking how a million soldiers could be kept alive without it. This was tantamount to saying that, at least so far as its principle was concerned, the system of Year II should have been maintained until the end of hostilities. But not a single Montagnard stood up to say so; nor did anybody utter the decisive words: runaway inflation, the *assignat* rendered worthless, the Republic reduced to bankruptcy. Objections were answered with self-contradictory arguments of incredible frivolity or naïveté. Beffroy, one of the most ardent advocates of controls in 1793, said:

> Once the *maximum* has been abolished, you will be able to hand over to private enterprise the supplies for our armies and the transport involved. . . . Then your expenses will be enormously reduced and you will no longer be forced to increase the number of *assignats* in circulation at such a revolting rate.

Réal declared: "The people are wise and will not demand the impossible." And Cochon said: "We are sailing between two reefs: having nothing or paying dear; the latter is better than the former; it is best to choose the lesser of two evils." The Convention was eager to cut down its expenses and to reabsorb the paper money, but it is hard to believe that it deceived itself; the more or less distinterested conviction that freedom would restore prosperity at the same time as profits, in conformity with the dogmas of political economy, and above all hatred for everything that came from the Montagnards—"Abolish an abominable law!" Bréard had cried—persuaded it to throw itself into the abyss. The law of 4 Nivôse, Year III (December 24,

1794) abolished the *maximum* and all controls. The peasants, in particular, became free again to sell at home and to circulate their produce without permit. As a transitional measure, the government confined itself to maintaining the market requisitions for two months and insisting on delivery of those which were in the process of being levied for the armies and for Paris. Finally the Trade Commission retained the right of pre-emption for the armies, on condition that it pay at current rates and take possession within a month.

Many other measures were required in order to put the principle into practice, and, as could have been foreseen, it was external trade which benefited most of all. As early as 2 Nivôse, Johannot had presented the report which served as the basis of the law of the thirteenth (January 2, 1795): it restored complete economic freedom and promised to reduce customs duties to mere nominal levies sufficient to cover the cost of trade statistics, a promise which was fulfilled on 12 Pluviôse (January 31); at the same it raised the sequestration of the property belonging to the other belligerents, a measure which indicated its intention to resume trade with them through the medium of the neutral countries, and which was also extremely profitable for Thérèse Cabarrus' father; on 20 Germinal (April 9), the ban on English goods would be maintained, but those which the merchants had managed to release from sequestration were allowed to be sold, and in point of fact the neutrals would henceforth import them without let or hindrance. On 3 Pluviôse (January 22), the Committee of Public Safety had revoked the requisitioning of foreign bills and securities; on the twenty-third (February 11), it rescinded the decree of 23 Ventôse, Year II, which had permitted the merchants of the great trading centers to export a host of various goods and had exacted payment to the Treasury of securities to a corresponding amount; as early as 2 Nivôse, as was only right and proper, the group to which Perregaux belonged had been dissolved and paid off; on 3 Germinal (March 23), it was confirmed that the circulation of foreign bills was free.

Internal trade benefited to a lesser extent. True, on 29 Pluviôse (February 17), the Committee recalled that the *maximum* for transport had been abolished; on the fifth (January 24), it had tried to revive the coasting trade by a secret decree admitting the neutrals to it, and by authorizing French ships to cover themselves with a false neutrality; it also raised several requisitions such as those of the eighth pig, of cast metal, of the oats required for the provisioning of Paris, and of 110,000 barrels of wine for Guinea; it gradually sold off the contents of the warehouses, which were henceforth useless; the armament factories closed down little by little or were handed back to private enterprise; and on 11 Pluviôse (January 30), it had decided to enter into contracts for the *service des étapes*, in other words for the provisioning of troops on the march. But it could not think of everything: it was only 14 Thermidor (August 1), that it remembered to raise the requisitioning of shipping; and since the need was great, the authorities resorted more than once, not only to pre-emption, but also to requisitioning, to which carters, bargees and workers concerned with charcoal and timber-floating remained theoretically liable; in Ventôse, 141,000 quintals of grain were commandeered for the armies in the west, and in the same month they were authorized to requisition fodder. The peasants were forced to complete the quotas previously laid down for the armies; on 12 Pluviôse (January 31), the Supplies Commission received an order to fix new quotas for Paris and the armies, and the requisitioning of markets was prolonged from month to month until 1 Messidor. What is more, the agents of the Supplies Commission had been instructed to make purchases for Paris on 14 Nivôse (January 3, 1795), and for the armies on 18 Pluviôse (February 6); as they were armed with the right of pre-emption, they disturbed the free operation of trade.

Finally, on the point which the financiers regarded as the most important of all, the Convention had not capitulated. On 17 Nivôse (January 6), acting on a proposal made by the Committee of Trade, Agriculture and the Arts, it had abolished the Commission of Trade and Supplies, but had simultaneously re-established it, calling it the Supplies Commission, in order to make it clear that it was giving up economic government—or as Boissy d'Anglas put it, abandoning the attempt to turn France into "a corporation of monks." It stipulated that the functions of the new body, as stated in a decree of the Committee of Public Safety on 4 Ventôse (February 22), were "not so much to direct the trade of the Republic as to safeguard the supplies which it might require," in other words to keep the armies provisioned; it was to the same end that on 22 Nivôse (January 11), control of the customs was taken away from it and transferred to the Commission of National Revenue. As a result the number of its agencies was reduced from eight to three. But one of these was specifically entrusted with purchases, which meant that the Convention did not intend to follow Beffroy's advice and hand over to the commissaries the responsibility for supplying the armies.

Meanwhile the Trade Council remained in existence;

it was abolished on 4 Ventôse (February 22) only to be re-established under the name of the Trade Bureau, now attached to the Committee of Public Safety and increased to fifteen members, one of whom was naturally Perregaux. The new commission was soon as discredited as its predecessor. It agents were held responsible for the rise in prices; and not without reason, since they paid any price to carry out their orders and competed with one another. On 6 Ventôse (February 24), in answer to complaints from Garnier de Saintes, Cambon put through a decree ordering that they all be recalled and forbidding the Commission to send any more out. But how was it possible to dispense with them? On the contrary: now that it was easy for them to leave the service in abeyance on the pretext that they could not find any sellers, the government had to give them a financial interest in their purchases by restoring their commission which Bouchotte had abolished; on 23 Ventôse (March 13), they received six sous for each quintal of grain, retroactively effective from January 1, 1793; the cost of the service increased by this amount. At the same time, on the pretext of pressing need, they bought without orders, thus exposing themselves to the suspicion of speculating for their own benefit, while representatives and war commissioners also placed contracts: in Messidor, the Committee of Public Safety quashed Beffroy's contracts for the armies of the Alps and Italy, and canceled the permits the representatives had granted to the war commissioners of the armies of the North and the Sambre and Meuse. However, it seems that, as under the *ancien régime,* it was the poverty of the Treasury which forced the government to give in: on 6 Ventôse (February 24), the Supplies Commission was authorized to accept tenders for the transport of fodder for the armies, and on the same day it placed a contract for the supply of the horses and mules needed for military transport, with a company directed by Lanchère, a well-known old commissary who, among other associates, had taken on Cerf Berr, a Strasbourg Jew who enjoyed a similar notoriety; on the third, a decree had forbidden the Transport Commission to make any purchases. This represented an initial success for the financiers, but nearly a whole year was to go by before the contractors had won the game and could pillage the Republic, so great was the reluctance of the Thermidorians themselves to abandon it to them.

However, the disaster was already obvious. On 8 Nivôse (December 28, 1794), a proclamation issued by the Convention had told the French people that the abolition of the *maximum* would be a source of blessings. "I should like it," Bentabole had nonetheless remarked timidly, "to contain a request to tradesmen not to take advantage of this law to crush the poor." As might have been expected, it took only a few days to reveal that prices were rising by leaps and bounds. In Paris, a pound of butter cost three livres at the end of Nivôse; two months later, it had doubled in price. Meat did not cost more than forty sous on 1 Pluviôse (January 20); it cost seven livres, twenty sous on 12 Germinal (April 1). Horrified, the Committee of Public Safety could not think of anything better to do than institute an inquiry into prices, on 20 Pluviôse (February 8)—which constitutes a valuable source of information but nothing more—and re-open the Stock Exchange on 13 Ventôse (March 3), under the pretext of cleaning up the market by making clandestine dealings useless. Speculation in essential foodstuffs increased to a fantastic extent, and Tallien, who needed a great deal of money, is said to have speculated in soap and candles, and also probably in *assignats* and currency. The depreciation of paper money was greater than ever in relation to metallic currency, although dealings in the latter were still forbidden, and above all in relation to the rate of exchange since international trade had been resumed. In frontier regions like the Haut-Rhin, close to Basle and Mülhausen, it was particularly debased. On an average, the violation of the *maximum* had made paper money lose a third of its value from July to December, 1794: it had fallen from thirty-one to twenty per cent. At the beginning of Germinal, it was worth only eight per cent at the most. The rise in prices was out of proportion with the increase in paper money, because the producers were unwilling to sell except in return for metallic currency, and were counting on an indefinite rise in prices and on bankruptcy.

The rise in prices did in fact condemn the Republic to inflation, all the more so in that the taxation system was working badly. In Year II, the French people had not paid many taxes, the *patente* had been abolished in 1793 and the land tax for 1794 was fixed only at the end of the year by the Thermidorians; moreover, the latter also abolished the personal tax; arrears would come in only slowly, and in the form of worthless *assignats*. There was a lot of talk about economizing, and it was partly in order to save money that the manufacture of arms was stopped and the number of government officials reduced. But the rise in food prices made it necessary to increase wages in the course of Nivôse and Pluviôse, and the members of the Convention themselves raised their daily emolument from eighteen to thirty-six livres on 25 Nivôse (January 14), effective retroactively from 1 Vendémiaire, a measure which created a scandal. Already there was no lack of people who could see no solution but the demonetization of the *assignat*: it would not be used except for paying taxes or buying national property, and the country would go back to using metallic currency. They forgot to add that this would produce a deflationary crisis, that it would hinder the revival of trade, the natural consequence, so it was said, of the return to economic freedom, and that as a result it would reduce even further the revenue from taxation. Moreover, how was the war to be financed, since it was obviously impossible to raise any loans? Demonetization was the ardent wish of the speculators, who hoped by monopolizing the *assignats* to lay their hands on what national property there remained, and of the enemies of the Revolution, who were counting on it to complete the discredit of the Convention in the eyes of the public. Cambon, the Montagnards and the Thermidorians who had remained Republicans therefore repudiated it, so that it became the bone of contention between the parties, and could not triumph until the Left had been finally crushed. In Pluviôse, there was talk of trying a loan in the form of a lottery, life annuities and tontines, or even of resorting to a complusory loan. But in his reports of 3 Pluviôse (January 22) and 7 Ventôse (February 25), Cambon laid particular emphasis on the rapid sale of national property and on the speeding-up of payment for it. In Ventôse, it was decided in fact that the purchaser should henceforth pay a quarter of the price within a month and the rest in six years, with the right to a bonus if he discharged his debt before 1 Vendémiaire; previous purchasers were granted the same favor, and measures were taken to speed up the sale of chattels. But the mass of *assignats* which it was hoped to reduce by these measures was increased during this time by continued issues. At the end of 1794, the total number of *assignats* was less than ten billion, of which eight billion are admitted to have been in circulation; between Pluviôse and Prairial, in four months, seven billion were printed and it is believed that the number in circulation rose to 11.5 billion. There was no remedy for the disease.

Everybody therefore tried to get rid of his paper money, and the flight from the *assignat* lowered its value to a far greater extent than the increase in circulation. From November 1794 to May 1795, the latter rose by 42.5 per cent, while the Treasury tables, based on the value of the precious metals, registered a drop in the value of 100 livres in paper money from 24 to 7.5 livres, in other words of sixty-eight per cent; at Basle, the exchange rate varied between twenty-seven and twenty-five livres in November and between nine and seven in May, which shows a more or less comparable fall. The *assignat* was so unpopular that in a department such as the Haut-Rhin it stopped being accepted immediately after the abolition of the *maximum*.

It should be noted, however, that in order to understand the effect of the depreciation on living conditions, it is by the price of foodstuffs and goods that it must be measured, rather than by the value of precious metals and foreign bills. When, in Year V, a depreciation table was drawn up in each department, it seems indeed that it was usually prices which were taken as a basis. It emerges from these figures that, on an average, 100 livres in paper money were worth thirty-two livres in November and eleven livres in May, which represents a fall of sixty-four per cent; it varied a great deal between one department and another, and the variation has been estimated at 110 per cent. But this rectification made by the local tables is in fact deceptive in that they have taken into account the market value of property, which had increased much less than the price of food. Mr. Harris, in his study *The Assignats*, estimates that the property index in March–April, 1795, had not risen above 439 in comparison with 1790, whereas the index of the prices noted in the Committee of Public Safety's inquiry stood at 758, and for foodstuffs alone at 819; at that date, the *assignat* index, on the basis of seventeen livres of metallic currency for 100 livres of paper money, stood at 581. Consequently the rise in the prices of basic essentials was far greater than the monetary depreciation would suggest, and from the social point of view, that is what matters.

The rise in prices was accompanied by a growing scarcity of food, because the peasant was reluctant to part with his grain. Yet it was he who had benefited least of all from the law of 4 Nivôse; as usual, he had been sacrificed to the towndwellers; up till 1 Messidor (June 19), he was subjected to market requisitioning; as far as Paris was concerned, twenty-five districts, at the beginning of Nivôse, owed a balance of 281,000 quintals out of the quota called for in Thermidor, Year II; thirteen others had to supply 87,000 quintals every ten days from 1 Nivôse; on the seventh (December 27, 1794), another thirteen districts were called upon to supply over 1,500,000 quintals up till 1 Messidor. In the provinces, all the district authorities lost no time in making similar demands for the benefit of their own markets. But as the peasants were now permitted to sell at home, they were slow to obey, and emptied their granaries either for the agents of the Supplies Commission who bought for the armies, or for the dealers who supplied the well-to-do. As early as 3 Pluviôse (January 22, 1795), the Convention authorized the arrest of recalcitrant peasants, but only on the authority of the representatives on mission, and subject to the allowances which the latter might grant—so that this decree came to nothing. The districts took it upon themselves to send National Guards to install themselves in the villages as bailiffs, in order to extract the indispensable grain from the peasants, and throughout the winter the latter were subject to military distraint. At the beginning of spring, it had to be admitted, even in the most fertile regions, that no further results could be obtained: the harvest had been too poor, and, since the peasants had succeeded in surreptitiously getting rid of their available stocks, they were left with just enough to live on until harvest time. At the beginning of Germinal, 700,000 quintals of the quota promised for the capital were missing; Versailles was no longer receiving any supplies from the Eure; in the district of Bergues, not a single grain came from the country after the end of Ventôse: the local authorities recalled the troops on 10 Germinal (March 30), and the markets of towns like Bergues and Bourbourg, which had always been well stocked in Year II, were henceforth completely deserted. The situation was almost the same at Orléans, at the gateway to the Beauce. As for the south of France, which in normal times was always short of food, its situation had been disastrous as early as the beginning of the winter.

While trying to share resources equitably among the various regions of France, the Committee of Year II had been obliged to buy outside: this represented the Thermidorians' last hope. Their first thought was for the south of

France. As early as 20 Brumaire (November 10, 1794), an agent had been sent to Montpellier to organize, either through trade channels or on the State's account, the export of wine to Genoa in return for grain; on 18 Frimaire (December 8), Toulouse was authorized to export 600,000 livres' worth of goods, and was given an advance to that amount with which to buy an equivalent return in the form of grain; on the twenty-sixth (December 16), Bayonne obtained six million livres for direct purchases; on 11 Nivôse (December 31), Cadroy and Expert were granted six million livres for advances to merchants willing to export, on condition that they imported corn in return, and Cadroy, having failed to obtain their help, set up a supply bureau which, in Ventôse, had already received thirty-five million livres from Paris and was consequently entrusted with the task of supplying the southern departments. The department of the Hérault created a similar body and requisitioned the brandies of the region for its benefit—a measure which, incidentally, it was hurriedly ordered to revoke. After the law of 4 Nivôse, the Committee of Public Safety showed a readiness to generalize the system in order to encourage purchases, without undertaking these itself: on 16 Pluviôse (February 4, 1795), it authorized the Supplies Commission to grant advances to districts which applied for them; in point of fact, the poverty of the Treasury obliged it to refuse these advances, and finally, on 30 Germinal (April 19), a decree decentralized purchases completely, making them the exclusive responsibility of the municipal authorities, which had to raise the necessary funds by freely subscribed loans.

These circumstances helped effectively to re-establish the preponderance of the upper middle class, for it alone was capable of providing the essential funds, especially as these had to be in metallic currency. A golden opportunity was also provided for those members of the upper middle class who, having emigrated, had settled abroad; their help had to be invoked to open credit accounts; the Protestant bourgeoisie thus served as a link between Nîmes and Genoa. But for Paris as for the armies, the State had to resign itself to making purchases itself by sending agents abroad and by making contracts either with French merchants such as Cerf Zacharias, who on 30 Pluviôse (February 18) undertook the feeding of the armies of the Rhine and the Moselle, or with the exporters of Amsterdam, Hamburg and Copenhagen. It also reserved Belgium for itself, and on 18 Floréal (May 7) banned all exports to that country without its permission. But consignments of grain only began arriving in large quantities after Floréal, especially in the north, where the main contracts dated from Prairial. The neutrals and particularly the Americans offered their cargoes spontaneously; in Ventôse, twenty ships docked at Bordeaux; others brought nearly 50,000 quintals to Le Havre in Germinal. In short, the purchases made abroad served essentially to help the country to get through the summer.

There was considerable suffering. At the time of the *maximum*, the French people had had cause to complain of the scarcity of foodstuffs; now they had to endure a serious shortage and even famine, and were faced at the same time with high prices. At Nantes, Madame Hummel, a draper's wife whose account book has been analyzed by M. Gaston Martin, had bought regularly from the baker until Pluviôse: from then on she received no more bread, and had to strain her ingenuity from day to day to find some flour which she had kneaded and baked; she was even reduced to eating biscuits. The plight of the poorer classes is easy to imagine. At Amiens, at the beginning of Germinal, the bread ration had not been more than three quarters of a pound for three months; since the summer of Year II, the municipality of Verdun had given only one pound to the workers and three quarters of a pound to others: at the end of Ventôse, Year III, it reduced this ration by half. At Toulouse, the price of bread had suddenly risen from five sous to eleven, immediately after the law of 4 Nivôse; the same thing happened at Verdun, where it rose at the end of Ventôse to twenty sous. The result was that in the towns controls became increasingly strict; the last municipalities which had succeeded in avoiding them were nearly all obliged to comply with them; Dunkirk, for example, finally resigned itself, on 7 Ventôse (February 25), to the mixing of grains and the distribution of ration cards.

The most unfortunate of all were the day laborers in the country: the towns had stopped giving them anything since their markets had disappeared, the rural municipalities rarely helped them, and they had to go from farm to farm begging the farmers to sell them food at an exorbitant price in order to keep their families alive. In the towns, at least, the authorities usually sold bread below cost price, for fear of riots. Gradually crowds began to gather again in the country, to prevent the departure of the grain or to loot the convoys.

The capital, which was supplied by the government, was in a privileged position. It was provided, not only with bread, but also with meat, wood, coal, candles and soap, at prices which had increased by a third on 22 Nivôse

(January 11), but which remained far below those current elsewhere. Consequently a great many people made for Paris to take advantage of this situation, and soon a housing crisis was added to the prevailing poverty. Even fraud was not uncommon. On 15 Pluviôse (February 3), the Committee of Public Safety had ordered a census and a complete change of ration cards: by the end of Germinal the operation had not been completed. For most foodstuffs, distributions were small and irregular, and taking into account this deficiency which obliged people to buy at current prices, Mr. Harris has calculated that the cost-of-living index must have risen in Paris from 580 in January to 900 in April. At least there was bread until the end of Ventôse, although queues at the bakers had formed again several times at the end of Nivôse and about 10 Ventôse. As early as Pluviôse, transport had ceased to be reliable. At Luzarches, Corbeil, and Soissons, mobs threatened grain deliveries on their way to the capital, and representatives had to be sent on special missions to safeguard them. Finally, on 24 Ventôse (March 14), the supply of bread failed completely, and the following day a decree reduced the ration to one pound, except for manual workers who were allowed a pound and a half. But on the twenty-ninth (March 19), the Committee of Public Safety wrote to the representatives that it had only 2,390 sacks left, from which 1,900 were being deducted for that day: "You will understand that we may well go without bread one day, but that we shall no longer have any control over the consequences. Think and act." On 3 Germinal (March 23), it requisitioned one fifth of all the grain and dried vegetables in the departments set apart for the provisioning of Paris and the armies, then, on the fourth, everything over and above the local consumption for two months within a radius of fifty miles. On the fifth, there were only 115 sacks left in stock; on the seventh, it gave instructions for the ration to be made up at the rate of three ounces of biscuits or six ounces of rice for half a pound of bread; but there was no longer any wood or coal over which to boil the rice.

The common people had made no attempt to save the Montagnards and the Jacobins from being outlawed. Now, exasperated by hardship, they stirred once more.

CHAPTER SEVEN

The Journées of Germinal and Prairial; the White Terror

It was customary for the people of Paris, especially since 1789, to display their anger every time there was a shortage of bread—unless the government inspired their respect, which was certainly not the case in 1795. On 27 Ventôse (March 17), delegates from the Faubourg Marceau and the Faubourg Jacques appeared before the Convention and declared: "We have no bread. We are on the verge of regretting all the sacrifices we have made for the Revolution." Greeted with an uproar, they retired shouting: "Bread! Bread!" and rejoined the crowd surrounding the Tuileries. On 1 Germinal (March 21), it was the turn of the Faubourg Antoine. On the seventh (March 27), several Sections held illegal meetings and rioting broke out at the Gravilliers; on the tenth, the section meetings were stormy, and on the eleventh, the Faubourgs once again appeared at the bar. The *journée* of the twelfth of Germinal only put the finishing touch to this gradual mobilization of the masses.

If these disturbances took a threatening turn, it was because the shortage of food coincided with a political crisis, as had happened several times since 1788. The Constitution of 1793 was in serious danger. The Commission of Sixteen set up on 31 Frimaire, after giving its attention to the so-called organic laws, had declared on 25 Ventôse (March 15) that it was abandoning the task, and on 10 Germinal it was decided to entrust it to another commission: as Ballieul and Thibaudeau had openly attacked the Montagnard constitution, the decree seemed ominous. Then again, on 2 Germinal discussion had begun of the indictment of the "Four"—Barère, Billaud, Collot and Vadier. Their former colleagues defended them courageously, especially Lindet and Carnot, who recalled the Convention to a sense of its own dignity by pointing out that it had approved the Committees of Year II: "On all occasions you did what you had to do; you could not have followed a different course without shattering the foundations of the democratic system to which you had sworn loyalty." And all of a sudden, on the eighth, Merlin de Thionville proposed that the trial should be referred to the future legislative body, the election of which was to begin on 10 Floréal (April 29): this was putting into effect that Constitution of 1793 which the reactionaries wanted to have done with, and, to explain this step, it must be assumed that Merlin no longer had any hope of obtaining the indictment of the Four, while in the existing situation in France he was convinced that the elections would insure victory for the Right. But the Committees secured the rejection of the motion and it was agreed to continue with the hearing of the accused. In the meantime, another great trial, that of Fouquier-Tinville, had opened on the eighth, before the revolutionary court.

In spite of the Thermidorians' accusations, there is no reason to believe that the Montagnards fomented a *journée* in order to save the terrorists; as for the members of the Sections, they did not mention the names of the accused, either because their leaders had no sympathy for them, or more probably because the people were not interested in deciding between the warring deputies. But it was a different matter for the Constitution, which was the symbol of democracy; its application had been an essential item of the program of the Hébertists, whom the *sans-culottes* had always regarded as their spokesmen; on the tenth, the Indivisibility Section called for it, and on the eleventh, the Quinze-Vingts demanded an elected municipality. It was on this point that the members of the Sections and the Montagnards may have come together; Léonard Bourdon is said to have stirred up the people at the Gravilliers; Vanheck, who acted as spokesman on 12 Germinal, was the agent of Dobsen, Thuriot's friend. We know little or nothing about the activity of the popular agitators, and it is impossible to state with any certainty that they combined together to stir up the Sections.

The Thermidorians were so sure that a *journée* was going to take place that Dyzès and Choudieu have accused them of having provoked it. The leaders of the *jeunesse dorée* had called on it to go into action once more. On 27 Ventôse, its bands, "in file and four abreast," tried to break up gatherings in the streets; they obtained control of several Sections which, on the eleventh and in the morning of the twelfth, came and harangued the Convention. For their part, the Committees tried to organize resistance. On 1 Germinal (March 21), Sieyès had a police law passed which laid down the death penalty for those who came to the Convention in a concerted movement and uttered seditious cries; arrangements were made for the National Guards of the Sections to be called in, and even the armies, in the event of the "oppressed" national assembly having to move to Châlons. But it would have been preferable to have troops near at hand; the Committees had only some National Guards from the prosperous districts of Paris at their disposal and were taken by surprise before they were called up. According to Duval, the *jeunesse dorée* was summoned, on the eleventh, to assemble the following morning in the courtyard of the Louvre, whence Tallien and Dumont led it to the Tuileries.

On 12 Germinal (April 1), the session of the Convention was interrupted by a crowd which invaded the chamber with cries of "Bread! Bread!" and created a prolonged uproar. Vanheck, at the head of the Cité Section, imposed silence and demanded the application of the Constitution of 1793, measures to deal with the shortage of food, and the release of the imprisoned patriots. The demonstrators finally allowed themselves to be persuaded, by the Montagnards themselves, to march past the bar and evacuate the chamber. In point of fact, it is impossible to talk of an insurrection organized by the Sections; two of them, indeed, in respectful addresses, expressed themselves to the same effect as the Thermidorians. It is therefore obvious that the movement had no leaders worthy of the name, and that the agitators, launching forth into speeches, had been unable to reconstruct the bands which in the past had insured the success of the *journées*. The demonstrators were unarmed; they had repulsed the *jeunesse dorée* easily, but when the National Guards of the western Sections, led by Merlin de Thionville, appeared, they withdrew without offering any resistance. However, the city was seriously disturbed; the Panthéon and Cité Sections declared themselves in permanent session; when Auguis and Pénières went to their headquarters, the former was arrested and wounded and a shot was fired at the latter. On the thirteenth, the agitation continued at the Quinze-Vingts. In the preceding night, the Convention had placed Paris under martial law and given command of the city to Pichegru, who happened to be there at the time, detailing Merlin de Thionville and Barras to assist him.

This pitiful scuffle immediately gave the Right the upper hand. The "Four" were finished with on the spot, during the night of the twelfth: in violation of the law of 12 Brumaire, they were deported without trial to Guiana and were promptly sent off on their way to the Île d'Oléron, with the exception of Vadier who had still not been arrested. Then it was decided to decimate the Left: eight of its members, including Amar, Duhem, and Choudieu, were arrested and sent to Ham. On the fourteenth, Cambon was expelled from the Finance Committee, and on the sixteenth a warrant was issued for his arrest (he managed to escape to Lausanne) and that of eight others, including not only Levasseur and Maignet, but also two leading Thermidorians, Lecointre and Thuriot, who had recently defended the thirty-first of May. Then, on 21 Germinal (April 10), a decree which the reactionaries had been demanding for a long time ordered the terrorists to be disarmed throughout the Republic—a new Law of Suspects which gave an extraordinary extension to that of 5 Ventôse. On 17 Floréal (May 6), the trial of Fouquier-Tinville came to an end, and he was executed the following day with Herman and fourteen jurors of the former revolutionary court. That same day, Lebon was brought before a commission of twenty-one. Denunciations of the former representatives on mission began again. "The assembly is in honor bound," declared Durand-Maillane, "to have these complaints examined."

The Right also succeeded in getting the condemnation of the thirty-first of May followed through to its logical conclusion. On 22 Germinal (April 11) those citizens who had been outlawed after that *journée* were quite simply reinstated in their civic rights, even Précy, the Royalist leader of the Lyons insurrection; the decree of March 27, 1793, which had outlawed the enemies of the Republic, was similarly revoked; those outlaws who, having gone into hiding, had been placed on the list of émigrés were to have their names struck off that list without further ado. It was obvious that a host of émigrés who had never had anything in common with the Girondins would thus be able to return freely to France. The Convention also considered the question of the restitution of the property of convicted persons; on 1 Floréal (April 20), it authorized all those who asserted joint rights on the property of émigrés, notably their wives and children, to recover their share; their parents were given permission to divide their property in anticipated succession and to buy back that part of their inheritance which reverted to the State at the estimated price, unless a third party bid at least a quarter more. The Republic even granted them a preference legacy of twenty thousand livres and abandoned all claims upon any inheritance which did not exceed that value. Finally, it renounced, for the future, all inheritances which might fall open in favor of the émigrés.

The constitutional question was meanwhile becoming more urgent every day. On 27 Germinal (April 16), the departmental authorities recovered the powers of which the law of 14 Frimaire had deprived them and the attorney-general-syndics were reinstated. Two days later, Cambacérès finally produced the Committees' report on the drawing-up of the organic laws, and in place of the commission of seven set up on 10 Germinal, had a commission of eleven appointed to this end. So far the validity of the Constitution of 1793 had not been disputed; Sieyès himself, dismissing the Convention's vote as worthless, had declared that he bowed to the plebiscite. It was a different matter now: on 25 Floréal (May 14) the Republic Section denounced "the decemviral Constitution, dictated by fear and accepted under the influence of fear"; in the midst of an uproar, Larivière expressed formal approval. On the eleventh (April 30), Lanjuinais had declared that the institution of two chambers was indispensable.

Meanwhile, barely a month after the twelfth of Germinal, the Thermidorians of the Center were beginning to grow alarmed at the progress made by the reaction.. Reports were coming in from all sides that the émigrés and the non-juring clergy were returning in large numbers; in Floréal, the massacres at Lyons and Aix upset them. On the twelfth (May 1), Chénier, on behalf of the Committees, had a decree passed that émigrés and non-juring priests would be prosecuted if they did not leave France again before the end of the month, as would those who incited the restoration of the monarchy, a clause chiefly aimed at the journalists; a penalty of six months' imprisonment was laid down for anyone who offended against the law on religious worship, after a violent attack by La Revellière on clerical plots. On the sixth (April 25), the Convention had already decided to give a decision itself on the striking off of émigrés, and on the twenty-sixth (May 15), the return of the inhabitants of Toulon, taken away in 1793 by the English and the Spaniards, was bitterly denounced. But there was lively resistance. Tallien defended the freedom of the Press, inveighing against Chénier whom he blamed for his brother's death, and opposed any fresh interference in the religious question; Thibaudeau even suggested that it was advisable to hand back the churches. On the other hand, the Committees went on protecting by their inertia the representatives who had been denounced. The gap between the Center and the Right had therefore opened up again. A complete split might have occurred before long if the Republican Thermidorians had been able to persuade themselves that order was going to be maintained. But a fresh *journée* occurred to patch up the coalition.

The financial situation was deteriorating from day to day. The fall of Cambon had marked a turning point in the history of the *assignat*, and demonetization, openly advocated in the press and at the tribune, was meeting with less and less opposition. On 26 Germinal (April 15), Johannot's report declared in favor of it, and on 6 Floréal (April 25), by revoking the decree of April 11, 1793, which had forbidden dealings in metallic currency and the practice of

two prices, the Convention appeared to give official sanction
to the collapse of the paper money. But it remained to be
seen how it was to be liquidated and what was to take its
place. On the first point, Johannot was in favor of exchanging the *assignats* for promissory notes bearing interest and
redeemable in the form of national property; on the second
point, Dubois-Crancé proposed a tax in kind: Bourdon declared this to be impracticable, especially in the midst of a
food shortage, and suggested softening it, at least, by authorizing the payment in *assignats* of the value of the
grain demanded, calculated according to the 1790 prices.
This idea was going to be adopted before long, but for the
State to get something out of it, there had to be a decree
that the *assignat* would no longer be accepted except at
the current rate of exchange. The same Bourdon revealed,
with two other projects, that speculation was lying in wait
and had agents in the Convention. He attacked the demonetization of the *assignats* bearing the royal head, which
had been decided on in July 1793, and proposed that those
which had not been able to be exchanged within the pre-
scribed period should be accepted in payment for the property of émigrés: apart from the fact that this would increase
the mass of paper money in circulation, it was pointed out
that the speculators had bought these *assignats* cheap in
the expectation of a concession of this sort. A little later,
Bourdon also proposed that henceforth national property
should be sold without auction to the first applicant and on
a simple valuation: this measure, adopted the following
year by the Directory, would permit the pillaging of the
Republic's inheritance. The Convention came to no decision. A fresh report from Vernier, on 23 Floréal (May 12),
which incidentally contained nothing new, was debated,

but the first of Prairial arrived before anything had been done. Inflation therefore continued, as did the rise in prices.

As for food, it became increasingly scarce as the spring wore on. Disturbances multiplied all over France. In Paris particular attention was paid to those which broke out on 14 and 15 Germinal, at Amiens and Rouen, to shouts of "Long live the King!" and "Bread and a king!" At Vernon, Évreux, Dreux, Montdidier, Chantilly, Crépy and La Chapelle, rioters stopped convoys on their way to the capital. At the beginning of May, a fairly large quantity of grain, bought by the government in Belgium and Holland, arrived at Dunkirk, Ostend and Le Havre, while from Marseilles came news of the unloading of 300,000 quintals. To safeguard the transport to Paris of the grain from the north, Barras was given full powers, and subsequently Rouyer and Féraud were appointed to assist him; he came to an arrangement with Lanchère, who supplied him with 6,000 horses, and he obtained the services of 3,500 troopers to escort the convoys. But this assistance was not enough to provide the Parisians with the promised ration. "We are reduced to two ounces of bread, and sometimes to nothing," a correspondent wrote to Goupilleau de Montaigu on 21 Floréal (May 10). As a result, agitation had started again among the Sections. On 10 Floréal (April 29) the Montreuil Section declared itself in permanent session and called upon the others to follow its example in order to discuss the food problem. The Convention lost no time in annulling the seditious decree, but the following evening rioting broke out in the rue de Sèvres, where women brought the grain wagons to a halt. On the thirtieth (May 19), the Mutius Scaevola Section came in a body to ask for bread, and the police reported that in the Invalides Section the workers were planning to join those of the Faubourg Antoine. It was rumored that the demonetization of the royal *assignats* was going to apply to notes of less than five livres, which were chiefly in the hands of the lower classes; this set the seal on their exasperation.

A pamphlet, published in the evening of 30 Floréal (May 19, 1795) and entitled *Insurrection of the People to obtain bread and reconquer their rights*, gave the signal for the movement. This pamphlet, which was known as *The Plan of Insurrection*, provided the popular agitators with definite objectives, the first of which was expressed in a single word: *Bread!* Its political aims were expounded at greater length: the putting into practice of the Constitution of 1793, the election of a legislative assembly which should take the place of the Convention, the release of the imprisoned patriots. The people were asked to march in a body to the Convention on 1 Prairial. There can be no doubt about the preparation of the insurrection by the *sans-culotte* leaders. As early as 29 Germinal (April 18), Rovère had reported a plot to the Convention. Several plans for an insurrection seem to have been prepared, particularly by the incarcerated patriots in the prisons themselves. Brutus Magnier, former president of the Military Commission at Rennes, and a prisoner at Le Plessis in Paris, had written at the end of Pluviôse an *Opinion on the insurrection required to save the country*, which outlines the same program as the *Plan* of 30 Floréal.

As for the deputies of the Left, their attitude on the first of Prairial showed that they looked favorably on the movement, yet they did nothing to organize or direct it. Lacking leaders, it spent itself, like that of the twelfth of Germinal, in violent but chaotic demonstrations.

Once again, it had been foreseen, and Thibaudeau had done his best to put some life into the Executive. On 7 Floréal (April 26), he had proposed abolishing the Committee of General Security and concentrating all power in the hands of the Committee of Public Safety, which should be in direct control of the police, the military, and even the Treasury. This was more than Robespierre had asked for, and the reactionaries set up a loud protest. On the fifteenth (May 4), Daunou presented another project which did not appease them. Cambacérès intervened as a mediator: the Committee of General Security was retained, but the Parisian military force was entrusted to it; the Committee of Public Safety, increased to sixteen members, divided into four sections, was authorized to issue decrees over the whole range of its jurisdiction and to sanction expenditure in conjunction with the Finance Committee. There is nothing to suggest that the executive was any stronger as a result. When La Revellière joined the Committee of Public Safety on 15 Fructidor (September 1), the latter, he said, had fallen

> into complete dissolution . . . ; each of its members busied himself only with his own affairs and those of his friends or supporters; each part of the administration was exclusively entrusted to one of them. He directed it as he pleased. . . . As there was no co-ordination on the Committee itself, the administrative commissions for their part acted on their own, in isolation, as they wished and as best they could.

At moments of crisis, in Prairial and Vendémiaire, the best that could be done was to create, as in Germinal, a provisional executive of a few representatives supposedly placed in control of the military force. At least the Committees increased the latter. On 28 Germinal (April 17), the National Guard was reorganized, and the Committees re-established the grenadiers, the light infantry and the cavalry, admission to which involved expenses limiting it to the rich; however, by the end of Floréal, this decree had been implemented only in the western districts, and there to a very limited extent. Numerous detachments which were protecting the food convoys could be drawn at need from the environs of Paris. On 30 Floréal, moreover, two divisions of gendarmes arrived from the Army of the Rhine. However, the Thermidorian reaction was not popular with the troops, and the staffs themselves did not seem to be entirely reliable; on 5 Floréal (April 24), the Convention had given full powers to the Military Committee and, in point of fact, to Aubry, to purge the latter, but this operation had not yet been completed.

On 1 Prairial (May 20), the tocsin rang and the alarm was sounded in the Sections in the east and center of Paris; the assembly rooms and guardhouses were broken into and the weapons removed. Then the demonstrators, wearing on their hats or pinned on their jackets the seditious inscription: "Bread and the Constitution of '93," marched on the Tuileries. About two o'clock, they invaded the palace by way of the Pavillon de Marsan, on the rue Honoré side, and entered the Convention hall. They were cleared out, but at about half-past three they broke open the doors and burst into the hall in a body; in the midst of the uproar, Féraud, who had attracted the invaders' attention by the resistance he had put up against them, was knocked down and murdered; his head was then carried around on a pike. Mingling with the deputies, the *sans-culottes* shouted at the tops of their voices; some of them made proposals at the tribune but could not manage to make themselves heard.

The President, Vernier, and Boissy d'Anglas, who took his place for a while, did not dissolve the meeting, and the din went on until seven o'clock. There were not many rebels and they were nearly all unarmed. According to Duval, the *jeunesse dorée*, summoned from its homes, had assembled in the garden about two o'clock. "It was left there, I do not know why," he remarks. In a short time, Raffet, the commanding officer of the Butte-des-Moulins Section, was able to bring up part of the National Guard of the western districts. The Committees were in session and had not been threatened; they were able to communicate without much difficulty with the Convention office. Yet nothing was done to expel the rioters. "This is a mystery," writes Dyzès. It is hard to avoid the suspicion that the Convention was waiting for the Montagnards to compromise themselves before it took action.

About seven o'clock, Vernier asked the deputies to gather together on the lower benches in order to deliberate, and the mob made way for them. Then at last a few Montagnards went so far as to put forward the definite motions: Romme and Duroy, the permanence of the Sections and the election of their committees, the release of the imprisoned patriots and of the deputies arrested since 12 Germinal; Goujon, the appointment of an extraordinary Food Council; Soubrany, the abolition of the Committee of General Security, which should be replaced by a commission consisting of Duquesnoy, Duroy, Bourbotte and Prieur de la Marne. It was after eleven o'clock at night and Soubrany was still speaking, when Raffet and Legendre burst in through opposite doors, at the head of detachments of the National Guard. The demonstrators promptly fled without anyone standing in their way. Immediately afterwards, a storm of denunciations broke out. The arrest of the six deputies who had just compromised themselves, as well as that of six others, was decreed. They were sent off immediately to the Château du Taureau at Morlaix.

It was a quiet night, but at eight o'clock the tocsin rang again. The Convention had just outlawed the rioters arrested the previous day when it learned that the rebels had occupied the Hôtel de Ville. In the afternoon, the military force went there and found nobody in the building, but soon it was pushed back to the Palais Égalité by the Faubourg Antoine, which was joined by other Sections. The gunners and the gendarmes deserted. However, instead of routing the Thermidorian National Guards, the rebels halted and ten members of the Convention came to parley with them: at eight o'clock it was announced that the two sides had "fraternized." Some petitioners were allowed to appear at the bar, where they once again called for bread and the Constitution of 1793. Vernier embraced Saint-Geniez, their orator. The *sans-culottes* had let their last chance slip through their fingers.

On the third, the Convention placed Aubry and two other deputies at the head of the military force, over which Menon assumed command. Reinforcements came pouring in; however, in the afternoon, the mob released Féraud's murderer as he was being taken to the scaffold. During the night, the government obtained control of most of the Sections and had the Faubourg surrounded. In the morning of the fourth, the *jeunesse dorée*, burning to distinguish itself, advanced into the Faubourg Antoine, where it was cut off; no harm was done to it, and eventually it was able to beat a rather inglorious retreat. Threatened with bombardment, and destitute of arms, ammunition, and bread, the

Faubourg allowed itself to be occupied toward evening. Already, the Assembly had given orders for the shooting without trial, not only of those who were taken carrying arms, but also of those who were wearing emblems other than the cockade; it entrusted the repression to a military commission, and instructed the Sections to meet on the fifth in order to initiate the disarming or the arrest of the terrorists. "Decent people" once again invaded the general assemblies and the anti-terrorist repression grew in scope.

These *journées* were decisive. For the first time since 1789, the government had put down a popular insurrection by force of arms, and thus broken the mainspring of the Revolution; for the first time the Army had answered its appeal and broken the tacit pact which, since the fourteenth of July, had bound it to the common people of the *journées*. The gap would go on widening; the common people would not budge again until 1830, and the Army would gradually take control of the Republic for the benefit of its generals. The National Guard was once again reorganized on the twenty-eighth (June 16): workers were debarred from it unless they demanded to be enrolled; the majors were henceforth elected by the officers and sergeants. The gendarmerie of the courts and the two divisions of gendarmes actually in Paris had been disbanded as early as the sixth. On 9 Messidor (June 27), a Parisian police legion was formed, the prototype of the Municipal Guard; on 24 Thermidor (August 11), a police administration of three members was set up, which Bonaparte was to replace by the Prefect of Police. Stern repressive measures, which decimated and intimidated the *sans-culottes*, were taken. The Military Commission pronounced some thirty death sentences, two-thirds of them on gendarmes. In the meantime, the Sections decided on their own authority to disarm or arrest the terrorists and Jacobins. The Convention continued to purge itself. On 5 Prairial, the deportation of Billaud, Collot and Barère was revoked and they were committed to the criminal court of the Charente-Inférieure. Luckily for them, Billaud and Collot were already on their way to Guiana, and as for Barère, the Committees saved his life by forgetting him at Oléron. The same day, Pache, Audoin, Bouchotte and others were handed over to the criminal court of Eure-et-Loir. On the sixth, Pautrizel was arrested; on the eighth, at the news of a revolt at Toulon, a decree was issued for the arrest of Escudier, Ricord and Saliceti, accused of complicity, and of three others including Panis and Laignelot who had done so much for the reaction; not satisfied with this, Clauzel committed to the Military Commission the Montagnards who had compromised themselves on the first of Prairial, in spite of the protests of Lesage and Fréron themselves, who invoked the law of 21 Brumaire. Brought back from Morlaix, they were sentenced on the twenty-ninth (June 17), six of them to death and one—Peyssard—to deportation. As they were leaving the courtroom, the condemned men stabbed themselves, the weapon passing from hand to hand. Romme, Goujon and Duquesnoy fell dead; Duroy, Soubrany and Bourbotte were taken, bleeding, to the scaffold. These were the "martyrs of Prairial" whose memory remained green among democratic Republicans for a long time.

Meanwhile, on 9 Prairial (May 28), Larivière had demanded the expulsion of the members of the former Committees. Lindet, Jeanbon, David, Élie, Lacoste, Dubarran and Lavicomterie were arrested, as well as Bernard de Saintes. In spite of Larivière, Carnot was saved by a deputy

who cried: "He organized victory." The name of Louis du
Bas-Rhin was also set aside, and there was no more talk of
Prieur de la Côte-d'Or. The other representatives who had
been denounced were attacked in their turn by Durand-
Maillane on the thirteenth (June 1); nine were arrested, including Sergent, Dartigoeyte, Javogues, Mallarmé and Bau-
dot. Ruhl and Maure, who were also threatened, committed
suicide. A little later, on 22 Messidor (July 10), Lebon was
finally sent before the criminal court of the Somme.

As usual, the Right accompanied its acts of repression by
measures calculated to gratify its friends. On 12 Prairial
(May 31), the revolutionary court had been abolished; on
the 20th (June 8), the Convention gave up striking off
émigrés itself; the next day, it restored the unsold property
of convicted persons, with a few exceptions, and quashed
all sentences for federalism; on the twenty-second, those
who had been listed as émigrés after the thirty-first of May
were struck off in a body; on 18 Thermidor (August 5),
certificates of citizenship were abolished. The priesthood
also came in for its share. On 11 Prairial (May 30), Lanjuinais had the churches placed at the disposal of the faithful if they asked for them; they nonetheless remained the
temples of decadal worship and, what is more, the Roman
priests had to share the use of them with the constitutional
clergy; in order to be admitted to them, all had to make an
act of submission to the laws of the Republic before the
municipal authorities. The restoration of religious worship
immediately gained speed, but religious pacification was not
complete; in theory, religious demonstrations were still
forbidden outside the churches, as was the use of bells; the
simultaneum provoked continual conflicts; on the question
of submission, the Roman priests split up, as in 1792 in

connection with the "little oath," into *soumissionnaires*, who followed Ennery's example, and *non-soumissionnaires* who continued clandestine worship. The deportation of non-juring clergy was not revoked, but on 19 Fructidor (September 5), their unsold property was returned to their heirs.

As for the *assignat*, the crushing of the *sans-culottes* necessarily led to its condemnation. True, under the pretext of saving it, it was decided on 12 Prairial (May 31) to sell national property without auction, as Bourdon had proposed; the districts were promptly besieged by prospective buyers, since the first applicant had priority; as early as the twenty-seventh (June 15), the Convention, realizing that everything was going to be bought cheap, in return for worthless *assignats*, re-established bidding, except for Parisian real estate—an exception which seems significant. At that point it abandoned the *assignat* to its fate; on 3 Messidor (June 21), it established a "scale of depreciation": the issue was retrospectively divided into blocks of five hundred million, and each of these involved an increase of one quarter on all debts. Then efforts were made to create new resources. On 26 Messidor (July 14), a loan of a million livres was floated, the subscription for which went on until the end of 1795; on 2 Thermidor (July 20), half the land tax was demanded in grain or in *assignats* at the current food prices; on the fourth, the *patente* was re-established, and on the seventh, the *mobilière*. As none of this produced any funds for the moment, inflation continued in spite of everything; about four billion livres were now being issued every month; in Messidor, the *assignat* dropped to five per cent, and in Thermidor to three per cent.

In the provinces, the *journées* of Germinal and Prairial

had given a strong impetus to the White Terror. Most towns now had their *jeunesse dorée*, whom the authorities allowed to act very much as they pleased. At Le Havre, Hardy told the Convention on 6 Thermidor (July 24): "A youngster of seventy is at their head, and they include men of eighty, sixty and fifty; these people call themselves the youth of Le Havre and presume to give orders to the authorities, who are in fear and trembling before these new terrorists." No patriot was spared: Hardy, who had seen thirteen of his relatives outlawed, was nonetheless called a terrorist and a Jacobin. At Bordeaux, in Messidor, when an agitator was arrested in the theater, the "young men" were called in to release him. At Nantes, green cravats, black collars, and hair put up "in victim style" were, as in Paris, their identification marks. They laid down the law at Toulouse, under the direction of the former members of the Parlement. At Avignon, they had formed "a defensive league which met at a given signal"; the department of Vaucluse changed it into a paid departmental force. At Marseilles, the National Guard was partly composed of young men called to the colors under the first levy. Everywhere as in Paris, therefore, the reactionaries had leagued together to obtain control of the streets. However, the White Terror, like that of Year II, raged to a very unequal extent, according to the region. In the southeast, where the massacres had begun during the winter, it was appalling. Elsewhere, excesses of this sort were avoided and the reactionaries confined themselves to the police measures and the legal action which the Convention had authorized, even at Brest, Arras and Cambrai where there had been a great many executions but where the reaction was rarely bloody.

The authorities had had no need to do anything but turn

the terrorists' own Law of Suspects against them. During the winter, a certain number had been arrested, but quite often they had been released; under the law of 14 Frimaire, government officials affected by the purge could have been imprisoned, but generally this was not done; however, the decree of 5 Ventôse placed them under surveillance. The first really general police measure was the disarming, ordered on 21 Germinal, of all who had "co-operated in the horrors committed under the tyranny which preceded the ninth of Thermidor." This involved placing the persons involved under surveillance. But as a general rule, even in Paris, no great haste was shown in carrying out this measure; it was the *journées* of Prairial which gave the signal. They aroused a wave of feeling in the provinces, where people thought that the country was on the eve of falling once more under the dictatorship of the *sans-culottes*. The authorities accordingly started zealously disarming them. Sometimes the municipality called a public meeting, where the terrorists were denounced and private hates were given full scope; if by some chance the popular society was still Jacobin in character, the opportunity was taken to suppress it, as at Lille on 17 Prairial (June 5); often the people who were disarmed were imprisoned into the bargain. Numbers varied considerably, but were never large, except in Paris and the southeast.

Legal action was taken chiefly against the representatives' commissioners, district administrators, mayors and national agents, and members of the revolutionary courts and surveillance committees. Here again, the process of exclusion created in 1793 was turned against the terrorists. The representatives opened inquiries and arranged denunciations, either through administrative channels like Boisset in the

Ain and Saône-et-Loire, or through the Public Prosecutor,
like Boursault in the Mayenne; afterwards they would commit the accused to the revolutionary court, or more often
to the criminal court of the department, which conducted
trials in the revolutionary manner—in other words, without
a jury. In either case, the rules of criminal procedure laid
down by the decree of September 16, 1791, remained a
dead letter and the jury of indictment was not consulted.
However, until the summer, there do not seem to have been
many convictions. A few people are known to have been
condemned to irons in the Manche, the Doubs and the
Hérault. It is true that the judicial archives have yet to be
submitted to a methodical analysis.

On 17 Germinal (April 6), the jurisdiction of the revolutionary court was reduced to the crimes of emigration,
treason, support for the monarchy and forgery of *assignats;*
all the other trials connected with the Revolution were referred to the ordinary criminal courts, so that the normal
process was restored. The terrorists took advantage of the
decree. In the Mayenne, the judicial inquiry into the case
of the Huchedé Commission, which had been carried out
for months by the Public Prosecutor, had to be begun all
over again. True, on 20 Floréal (May 9), the Convention
did new violence to the law by authorizing administrative
bodies themselves to denounce terrorists to the police; it
repeated the offense several times by outlawing its own
members without trial and by referring to the criminal
courts, by decree, the terrorists of the Ardennes, the revolutionary court of Brest and the Jacobins of the Mayenne.
Since, at this time, the Convention was sending on mission
reinstated Girondins who put professed Federalists and Royalists into positions of power, the number of trials rose

steadily. In the Aube and the Marne, Albert ordered the municipalities to receive plaints; the municipality of Verdun went to great pains to put on trial the men who had sentenced the Federalist Delayant, and had the minute-book of the surveillance committee read out in public. The "young men" also tried to take the initiative; at Tours, they asked Pocholle to hand over to them the archives of the authorities of Year II. "It is the same everywhere," said somebody at the Convention, while Mailhe, speaking approvingly of the young men of Tours, demanded that the minute-books of the "infamous revolutionary committees" be inspected everywhere.

However, once these noisy denunciations had been recorded, the subsequent process was usually quite regular: the magistrate carried out the preliminary investigation and sent his file to the indictment jury. On examination, the indictment was generally found to be untenable: it was based on unfounded accusations, mere threatening remarks, acts in conformity with the law and with the representatives' decrees. At Reims, the indictment jury dismissed two charges and the trial-jury acquitted the other thirteen accused on 25 Vendémiaire, Year IV (October 17). The slowness of the preliminary investigation enabled many of the accused to benefit from the amnesty without having been tried; this was the case with the revolutionary court of Brest, the revolutionary commission of the Cantal, the terrorists of the Mayenne, and Pache and Bouchotte at Chartres. At Verdun, the efforts of the municipality— opposed by Pons, a member of the Convention and the brother of one of the accused—did not even lead to a prosecution. However, a few terrorists were sentenced to irons or imprisonment. The record office at Coutances is the only one whose files have been adequately examined in this respect: in the districts of Coutances, Valognes, Carentan and Cherbourg, the public prosecutor took action against seven people and administrative or private denunciations resulted in the prosecution of sixteen others; of these twenty-three accused, four were discharged, six were finally not tried, and nine were acquitted; thus only four were sentenced, one to irons and three to imprisonment. It is impossible at the moment to calculate the number of executions, but there do not seem to have been many. The most famous was that of Lebon, at Amiens, on 17 Vendémiaire, Year IV (October 9, 1795). Seven terrorists of the Ardennes had been guillotined on 28 Prairial (June 16). In the Marne, where the Septembrists of 1792 had also been prosecuted, two were put to death on 1 Fructidor (August 18). If matters had been left to the Thermidorian bands, much harsher measures would have been taken; on more than one occasion, they intervened to intimidate the witnesses and the court, or to start a riot in the event of an acquittal. In Thermidor, at Dijon, where a lieutenant of the gendarmerie, a former member of the surveillance committee, had been discharged under the motive clause, the authorities were forced to arrest him again, and Ysabeau got the Convention to commit him to the criminal court of the Haute-Saône with his fellow accused. It should be added that prosecution was somethimes accompanied by a civil action. At Rouen, a member of the surveillance committee, acquitted of the charge of arbitrary arrest, was nonetheless ordered to pay 10,000 livres in damages; at Troyes, the national agent, sued by a citizen whom he had taxed "in the revolutionary manner," was acquitted by the jury, but sentenced by the magistrates to restitution and a fine.

Moreover, these trials give only an inadequate impression of the ordeals inflicted on the terrorists. Everywhere they were subjected to countless annoyances; they were reduced to poverty and their lives were made unbearable; those who were able to do so moved to another part of the country in order to be forgotten.

Yet their sufferings were mild compared with those of their brothers in the southeast. At Bourg, toward the end of Germinal, the district persuaded the representatives on mission at Lyons to commit the terrorists, who had been in custody since Thermidor, to the criminal court of the Jura; on the thirtieth (April 19), as they were being taken out of the town, six of them were murdered. The murderers, who were prosecuted in Year VII, are known to us: they included some artisans and shopkeepers, but also a notary, a bailiff, the clerk of the criminal court, and a former secretary of the department. At Lons-le-Saulnier, the prison was broken into twice, on 6 and 7 Prairial, and three men died. For their part, the Jacobins of the Jura had been sent to Bourg, whence they were brought back on 13 Prairial (June 1): some masked men ambushed the convoy and killed ten of them. The public prosecutor had stirred up feeling with his speeches and none of the authorities had taken any precautions; the mayor later declared that the murderers belonged to the cream of society and were boasting about their exploit in the salons; the inquiry into the affair yielded no results. On the 16th, at Lons-le-Saulnier, two more Jacobins were attacked; one of them survived, only to be sentenced to irons on 19 Vendémiaire, Year IV (October 11).

At Lyons, the mass killings began again on 5 and 15 Floréal (April 24 and May 4). The second was the bloodier of the two: one of the city's prisons was set on fire and some of the inmates put to death, about a hundred it is said. Several of the murderers were masked; others were tried, acquitted and carried away in triumph; the National Guard had not lifted a finger to enforce law and order. The infection spread to the department of the Loire and raged furiously at Montbrison and Saint-Étienne, where the murders were embellished with tortures; several thousand workers fled into the woods and mountains.

In Provence, the Marseilles Company of the Sun went to Aix and, on 22 Floréal (May 11), massacred twenty-nine of the thirty accused in the Vendémiaire affair; on 27 Thermidor (August 14) another fifteen prisoners were killed. Toulon remained the last fortress of the Jacobins; a fresh insurrection provided an opportunity to subjugate it. On 27 Floréal (May 16), the municipality having decided to raise the price of bread as soon as the squadron had put to sea, the *sans-culottes* tried to prevent its departure and took up arms; one of the representatives in the town succeeded in getting the ships to put to sea, and the others fled. Having gained control of the town, the rebels marched on Marseilles; General Pactod routed them on 4 Prairial (May 23). These events, which were seen as an extension of the disturbances in Paris, filled the reactionaries with a bloodthirsty fury. At Marseilles, Chambon gave the Company of the Sun a free rein. On the 17th (June 5) it forced its way into the Fort Saint-Jean; the prisoners put up a spirited resistance, but eighty-eight of them died. At Tarascon, in the Château du Roi René, forty-seven Jacobins died in the nights of 5-6 Prairial (May 24-25) and 2-3 Messidor (June 20-21). If we are to believe Fréron, the members of high society installed themselves comfortably on the banks of the Rhône to watch the bodies being thrown from the towers into the river. Lambesc and Salon witnessed more murders; at Nîmes, Courbis and two of his companions were killed on 16 Prairial (June 4). Other prisoners were killed on the highway, thirteen during their transfer from Orange to Pont-Saint-Esprit on 8 Prairial (May 27). Individual attacks on Jacobins who remained at liberty continued throughout the summer. "Throats are being slit everywhere," Goupilleau wrote from Montaigu on 13 Prairial (June 1); people went patriot-shooting instead of partidge-shooting.

As for the *sans-culottes* of Toulon, the forces of the law had taken them in hand. On 8 Prairial (May 27), the Convention had set up a military commission for this purpose and committed the representative Charbonnier to trial as instigator of the rebellion. The Commission, to which Chambon had added a jury, showed a tendency to indulgence; consequently on 20 Messidor (July 8), Royer transferred it to Marseilles, where Isnard was absolutely pitiless. The jury was suspended and sentences were passed without delay: fifty-two to death and fourteen to other penalties. Nonetheless 152 of the accused had been acquitted and about a hundred benefited by the amnesty as did Charbonnier. The southeast also witnessed some trials before the civil courts; the best known was that of seven members of the Orange Commission who were executed at Avignon on 8 Messidor (June 26); at Marseilles, the terrorist Izoard was guillotined on 3 Vendémiaire, Year IV (September 25). In this region, the trials were nothing but farces. At Avignon, the preliminary investigation was carried out in public; the witnesses for the defense were not allowed to give evidence, and at the trial the defense counsel threw up their briefs.

At an early date, the White Terror began to worry the Thermidorians of the Center because they realized that it was aimed indiscriminately at all supporters of the Revolution. As early as 11 Prairial (May 30), Clauzel brought the operations of the Parisian Sections to a stop; in Messidor, Doulcet de Pontécoulant, an outlawed Girondin, called for "stern, prompt measures"; on the sixth (June 24), the Lyons authorities were suspended, the National Guard disarmed, and the military commandant charged with treason; that was enough to bring the Company of Jesus to its senses. But these measures were not extended to Provence, and there disorder continued. True, Mollevaut, another outlawed Girondin, had got an exceptional law passed on 30 Prairial (June 18), in the name of the Committees; this made murder a capital offense, abolished the intervention of the indictment jury, and insisted on a trial within twenty-four hours, without appeal. But in doing so he nearly played into the hands of the reactionaries. The Committee of General Security and the provincial authorities had begun releasing the imprisoned terrorists (of whom there were said to be 30,000) and the Sections were protesting. Taking up the defense of the law, the Right proposed the re-establishment of the indictment jury, but its project also ordered the prosecution, not only of the murderers of the south of France, but also of the Septembrists and the authors of "thefts, despotic acts, judicial murders and abuses of authority." The frightened Committees recoiled; Cambacérès restored unanimity by setting aside the new decree and getting Mollevaut's decree revoked. Everything accordingly went on as before; the White Terror continued, but the Committee of General Security was also able to release those terrorists who were not accused of any offense in common law, in spite of the Sections who had begun claiming the right to pronounce judgment on them.

If the reaction alarmed those Thermidorians who were still Republicans, it was because the Royalists were openly turning it to their account. Nearly all the papers now favored them. The *Moniteur* was one of the rare exceptions: "The most insane hopes are being expressed on all sides," Trovère wrote in it on 17 Prairial (June 5). "It seems that there is nothing left for the Convention to do but proclaim the restoration of the Monarchy." In the provinces, the trees of liberty were cut down and the tricolor cockade trampled underfoot. At Le Havre, the secretary of one Section had declared: "We want a king . . . to achieve that aim, we must make sure of England." Brought to trial, he had been acquitted, to the cheers of an armed crowd of "young men." At Bordeaux, Bresson wrote on 27 Messidor (July 15): "There is a party of avowed Royalists who are undoubtedly in communication with the other Royalists of the other large communes of the Republic." In Provence, Goupilleau was astounded at the progress they had made: "I am regarded as one of the biggest terrorists in the Republic; . . . to please those gentlemen, I would have to accept a post as major-domo to the Pope." There were rumors to the effect that a good many deputies were prepared to come to terms with them. Those mentioned included Boissy d'Anglas, who had given Lacretelle a post in an office; Aubry, who was hunting out Republican officers; Larivière, Cadroy and Chambon. In their letters, Louis

XVIII, Grenville and Mallet du Pan mentioned Tallien, Merlin de Thionville and Cambacérès.

But these members of the Convention could not give themselves up bound hand and foot; the Royalists were unable to agree on the concessions to be made to them. Some of them were Constitutionalists who would have been satisfied with a return to the Constitution of 1791, in a revised form; they would have governed on behalf of Louis XVII, who would have been released from the Temple and provided with a regency council. Outside, they had no lack of supporters: Archbishops Cicé and Boisgelin, Mallet du Pan and Calonne himself. But the boy died at a date difficult to establish, and Monsieur, the Comte de Provence— then installed at Verona with his loyal supporters d'Avaray and Saint-Priest—was not prepared to negotiate with the regicides. Having taken the name of Louis XVIII, he published on June 24 a manifesto in which he promised to punish them and to re-establish the three orders, the *parlements*, and the predominance of the Church. The Comte d'Artois, who had gone from Hamm in Westphalia to England, was no more conciliatory. In the entourage of the Princes, there was talk of hanging the members of the Constituent Assembly, shooting the purchasers of national property, and returning purely and simply to the *ancien régime*. At Verona, d'Antraigues, who was in the pay of the English, was reputed to be one of the most fanatical Royalists. The more moderate among them would not agree to anything more than a pardon for the Constitutional Monarchists. But, protested Mallet du Pan:

If, under the sword of the omnipotent Republicans, they worked at their risk and peril to obtain recognition for the

King, would they not consider themselves entitled to gratitude rather than pardon?

They were left with no option but to come to an agreement with the Republican Thermidorians to obtain a temporarily tolerable constitution.

The death of the young King Louis XVII [wrote Mallet du Pan on 21 June] is the most disastrous of events at this moment. It has dismayed and discouraged the Monarchists, insured the triumph of the Republicans, and guaranteed the success of the new gibberish which they are going to decree in the name of a constitution.

In his opinion, there was only one mistake which the Absolute Monarchists could make, and that was to resort once more to insurrection combined with invasion and treason.

There can be no hope of a spontaneous insurrection in Paris or anywhere else in favor of the Monarchy. . . . Civil war is a pipe-dream of the same sort. . . . The expedient of a foreign war is just as threadbare: there is nothing to compare with the contempt felt in France for the arms and policies of the Allies, unless it be the no less general hatred which they have inspired.

Yet such was the plan of the Absolutists. The Toulouse Royalists, wrote the representative Bousquet,

say that the Convention has helped them to achieve a better state of affairs, but that nonetheless it will be destroyed before long, that not one of its members will escape them, that they have enough people in Paris to cut all their throats, and that it will then be a simple matter for them to cleanse the earth of that mob of patriots who are all terrorists.

In Lozère, in the Haute-Loire and the Ardèche, and in Franche-Comté, the Royalists were trying to rebuild their insurrectional groups and were convinced that they could start a rebellion at the first news of invasion. From Switzerland, Imbert-Colomès was organizing a plot in Lyons. In Paris there existed a "Royal agency" which was financed by the English and included among its members the Abbé Brottier, the Chevalier des Pommelles, the former Lieutenant-Commander Duverne de Praile, the former Councilor of State La Villeheurnois, and Sourdat, a sometime police lieutenant at Troyes. On May 23, Montgaillard called on Pichegru, the general in command of the Army of the Rhine, on behalf of the Prince de Condé, who was encamped in the region of Baden, and returned on June 14 to offer him money and the rank of lieutenant-general. The Comte d'Artois had an agency too, in Jersey, where an attack on Saint-Malo was being planned. Finally, at the beginning of Prairial, the Chouans had taken up arms again to support the expedition which the English had at last announced as imminent. It was a bad time to choose, for the Coalition had never been in such a bad way. The Absolutists were rushing into an adventure which, as Mallet du Pan had foreseen, would turn to the advantage of the Revolution.

CHAPTER EIGHT

The Thermidorians
and the Coalition;
the Quiberon Disaster

After destroying the organization which had insured victory, the Thermidorians, at grips with the whole of Europe, were nonetheless saved by two lucky chances: they gathered the fruits of that same victory, and they saw the Coalition, which had been tottering for a long time, finally collapse.

At the time of Robespierre's death, Belgium had been reconquered; victorious at Fleurus on 8 Messidor, Year II (June 26, 1794), the Army of the Sambre and Meuse had entered Brussels, where Pichegru, after occupying Flanders, joined it with the Army of the North. From

Brussels, Jourdan had marched on Liège and Pichegru on
Antwerp: the two cities were reached on the same day, 9
Thermidor (July 27). However, the enemy's armies had
not been destroyed: Clerfayt retired behind the Roer and
the Duke of York into Holland; in the rear the French had
to recapture Valenciennes, Condé, Le Quesnoy, and Lan-
drecies. They also had to take control of the conquered territory; on 16 Thermidor (August 3), the Committee of
Public Safety forbade any attempt to "municipalize" it
and to repeat the experiment of 1792. It was placed under
military government and exploited to the utmost; nonetheless, military operations were delayed for a while.

This delay was a brief one because the fortresses in the
north capitulated much more quickly than had been expected, possibly as the result of a decree which had stipulated that no quarter be given to their garrisons if they
put up a prolonged resistance. In September, the armies
moved off again. The Army of the Sambre and Meuse
forced the passage of the Ourthe, then that of the Roer at
Aldenhoven, on 11 Vendémiaire, Year II (October 2,
1794), and pushed Clerfayt back beyond the Rhine, while
the Armies of the Moselle and the Rhine were invading the
Palatinate. Soon the French reappeared before Mainz
and attacked Mannheim, which surrendered on 4 Nivôse
(December 24); in the rear, they laid siege to Luxembourg,
which held out for a long time.

In the meantime the Army of the North was making
its way to the Meuse and was subjugating the Dutch fortresses, notably Maestricht. Pichegru showed no great eagerness to press on, but at the end of December, the harsh
winter opened the way for him: the rivers froze and the
Republicans crossed the Meuse, the Waal, and the Lek in

succession. As early as December 2, the Duke of York had set off for Hanover; the Prince of Orange set sail for England, and Holland was occupied almost without firing a shot; off the island of Texel, his fleet, trapped by ice, was seized by the hussars. The Dutchmen who had fled their country after the failure of the revolution of 1787 accompanied the Army of the North, and Daendels proclaimed the Batavian Republic. In the Alps, Carnot had abandoned the invasion plan proposed by Bonaparte and supported by Robespierre, and was on the defensive; near the Pyrenees, on the other hand, Dugommier had defeated the Spaniards at the Montagne Noire on 27 Brumaire (November 17); he was killed, but his army nonetheless descended into Catalonia, where it took Figueras and Rosas. In August, 1794, Moncey, for his part, had captured Fuenterrabia and San Sebastian. These victories, and above all the conquest of the Netherlands, were of prime importance to the Republic; the liberation of French territory and the moral effect in France and Europe were not the only advantages: the blockade, which in any case had never been complete, was finally broken as soon as France had the resources of the Netherlands and the left bank of the Rhine at her disposal and, by means of coasting vessels, could resume direct contact with Hamburg and the Scandinavians; in the conquered regions, the evacuation agencies, set up in Floréal, Year II, collected grain, cattle, cloth and metal, either for the use of the armies or for sending to France. Finally, Tuscany, Spain, and the Princes of Southern Germany henceforth showed themselves prepared to negotiate.

This was not the first sign of weakness revealed by the Coalition: Prussia was also showing a tendency to abandon it, and this was much more important. Her hesitations dated back a long time. When they had joined the war against France, the Germans had been agreed that they were to recoup themselves, and not simply at their enemy's expense: Austria had her eye on Bavaria, while Prussia had designs on Poland. Defeated at Valmy, Frederick William II had declared that he would only continue fighting if he could collect his rewards immediately, and since Catherine II, delighted at the opportunity to divide the Germans, had concurred in his views, Russia and Prussia had carried out the second partition of Poland on January 23, 1793. Thugut, the new Austrian Chancellor, had had to resign himself. The Prussians nonetheless fought very half-heartedly in the west, and in 1794, when the Poles rose in revolt, their King went and laid siege to Warsaw. However, things turned out badly; he was forced to raise the siege on September 6, 1794, and it was Suvoroff who recaptured the city; the Austrians took the opportunity to make it up with Catherine II, who allowed them to occupy Cracow and Sandomir. As a result the Prussians went back across the Rhine, and after Pitt had taken this as an excuse to cut off their subsidies, the King decided in November to send some agents to Basle to get in touch with Barthélemy, who represented the French Republic in Switzerland: he wanted to come to terms with France in order to take all his troops to Poland and force his rivals to admit him to the third partition which was being prepared. Sweden also served him as an intermediary: Baron de Staël set off to negotiate with the Thermidorians, and in December, Madame de Staël published her *Réflexions sur la paix.* Prussia's defection created a tremendous sensation. "The legalized victory of the Revolution," wrote Mallet du Pan, "will be a license for insurrection addressed to all the peoples of the world."

Frederick William II was well aware of this and had yielded only reluctantly to the arguments of his generals and his minister Haugwitz. He also foresaw that the regicides would demand the Rhine frontier, and was afraid that, in giving way to them, he would compromise Prussia's reputation in the eyes of all the Germans. Hardenberg, his other adviser, played on his reluctance, as did the English; he finally stuck to the decision he had made, after Russia and Austria had settled the final partition of Poland, on January 3, 1795—without consulting him, and reduced his share to the minimum. What is more, in exchange for his Rhenish possessions, Prussia was entitled to hope for some compensations in Germany; since on December 22 the Reichstag had declared itself in favor of peace, it was not impossible that the Princes should turn to her, if Austria continued the war, to form within the Holy Roman Empire a sort of confederacy designed to protect their neutrality under her direction. These were attractive prospects.

The Republic, for her part, also needed peace. Carnot had already said as much before the ninth of Thermidor, and the need had become much more pressing for the Thermidorians, who lacked both money and authority. Besides, the nation's wishes were not in doubt. "The most ardent and the most general feeling," noted Mallet du Pan, "is a desire to achieve some sort of end to the Revolution and to have done with the war." However, certain difficulties could be foreseen. The Committee of Year II could have negotiated for peace if it had thought fit, because it dominated the Convention and because it could not be suspected of coming to terms with the Royalists. The

Thermidorian Committee was in a very different position. When, on 22 Pluviôse (February 10), Cambacérès presented the treaty concluded the day before with the Duke of Tuscany, the Assembly showed an unexpected chilliness: having failed to consult it, the Committee seemed guilty of usurpation in its eyes, and it ratified the treaty only reluctantly. It was even worse on 13 Ventôse (March 3), when the Committee asked for authority to insert secret articles in future agreements. How could the Convention give its approval to articles when it did not know what those articles were? The Committee was obliged to explain that peace with Prussia depended on this condition. On the twenty-seventh, the required authority was granted, on condition that the secret articles should not attenuate the others.

The question of the annexations was even more delicate. At the beginning of 1793, the Convention had allowed itself to be persuaded to give the Republic its "natural frontiers" and, on the basis of hasty plebiscites, to annex Belgium and the left bank of the Rhine. It is unlikely that the Committee of Year II considered itself bound by these decisions. The Thermidorian Committee too realized that if it insisted on the Rhine as a frontier, it ran the risk of postponing a general peace indefinitely, and it maintained a prudent reserve. France, declared Merlin de Douai on 14 Frimaire, Year III (December 4, 1794), "will trace with her victorious but generous hand the limits within which it befits her to remain"; and on 11 Pluviôse (January 30, 1795), Boissy d' Anglas added that the Committee was ready to conclude a peace "consistent with our dignity and likely to guarantee our safety." The conditions of such a peace therefore remained to be discussed. But the counterrevolutionaries immediately started a campaign in favor of peace at any price and the return of all the Republic's conquests; and as early as 24 Brumaire (November 14, 1794), Barère had denounced the advocates of "a patched-up peace." The leaders of the *jeunesse dorée,* needing the Royalists, did not oppose them; on 14 Brumaire, Tallien stated that the only means of halting inflation was a peace which would "make us withdraw within our former limits." Gradually the Royalists and those who humored them became the party of "the former limits." This was enough to make the Thermidorians who had remained Republicans hesitate; besides, in their eyes it was playing the Jacobins' game to suggest abandoning the Republic's conquests, for the nation would not relinquish them without regret, however much it might long for peace; and as for the army, whose support was so essential to the government, there could be no doubt about its feelings on this score. On 8 Nivôse (December 28, 1794), Bourdon spoke out unequivocally: "There are some who want to squander the successes of our armies and waste the blood they have shed by confining you to your former limits. How can you hope to ruin England except by the conquest of the three rivers [the Escaut, the Meuse and the Rhine]?" And on 11 Pluviôse, he stated explicitly what Boissy d'Anglas had deliberately left uncertain: "We shall confine ourselves within the limits which Nature has set, beyond which all peoples shall be our allies." Thus, because of the weakening of the Executive, the basic problem that French diplomacy had to solve became a party issue, and gradually it became possible to measure the warmth of a man's Republican convictions by his attachment to the country's natural frontiers.

Meanwhile the Committee, informed of Prussia's offers, had asked her to send an agent to Paris, and on January 7, 1795, notified her that in signing a peace treaty she would have to agree in advance to the eventual cession of the left bank of the Rhine, in return for compensations to be decided later, but naturally in Germany; without compromising the future by public declarations, it therefore intended to reserve the decision for itself. The King, who would have preferred an armistice, agreed to negotiate, but as Goltz, his ambassador in Basle, had died, he sent Hardenberg to take his place; Hardenberg contrived not to meet Barthélemy until March 19, and raised a new difficulty by insisting that North Germany should be neutralized under a Prussian guarantee. The Committee took umbrage at this. On 15 Ventôse (March 5), Sieyès and Reubell had joined the Committee and had acquired considerable influence on it. Now it so happened that the Alsatian Reubell was an ardent annexationist, and Sieyès, like Dumouriez and Danton, wanted an alliance with Prussia against Austria; Hardenberg's demand ran counter to their plans and the Committee described it as an ultimatum. The Thermidorians of the Right worked themselves up into a fury. La Revellière recounted later how Rovère and Lanjuinais inveighed against Sieyès, "an ambitious character who sacrificed his country to his private opinions, opposed peace with Prussia and, having sold himself to Russia, wanted to sacrifice our northern allies and Turkey"; in order to damage his reputation, it was said that he had been the man who "made" Robespierre, and there was talk of taking diplomacy out of the hands of the Committee of Public Safety. But in the meantime the King decided to give way on the question of the Rhine, and Barthélemy,

catching the ball on the bounce, took it upon himself
to accept the neutrality of North Germany; the peace treaty
was signed during the night of 15-16 Germinal (April 4-5).
In any case, the Committee, threatened with an insurrection, had withdrawn its veto.

The agreement with Prussia led to the capitulation of the
Dutch, whose envoys, since their arrival on March 10,
had doggedly disputed the leonine conditions which
Sieyès and Reubell wanted to impose on them, counting on
the resistance of Frederick William II. It was in vain that
they pleaded that the Batavian Republic, founded by the
friends of France, was entitled to special consideration.
The Committee sent Sieyès and Reubell to The Hague,
armed with an ultimatum which shattered the Dutch resistance. By the treaty of 27 Floréal (May 16), France acquired Dutch Flanders, Venloo and Maestricht, which she
could not keep without annexing Belgium, so that another
mortgage had to be taken out on the future; she also occupied Vlissingen until the end of hostilities. Holland became her ally and agreed to maintain an occupation corps
of 25,000 men; she promised an indemnity of 100 million
florins and reimbursement of the *assignats* which the conquerors had distributed throughout the country, to the
value of about thirty million florins. The French had taken
an advance on the indemnity, which was estimated at ten
million florins, by levying a succession of requisitions; the balance was to be paid in currency and in bills which the Committee hoped to discount at banking centers in the vicinity
of France. But it was the Directory which benefited most
of all by this agreement: in September, out of the twenty
million florins which had fallen due, Holland had paid only

11.25 million, of which less than five million were in currency.

The peace with Spain was delayed for a while, because Godoy had cherished some fantastic illusions, proposing the creation of a kingdom for Louis XVII in the south of France and the restoration of the privileges of the Catholic Church; for its part, the Committee wanted to annex Guipuzcoa and the Spanish part of Santo Domingo, recapture Louisiana, win over Spain as an ally and make her attack Portugal, in order to wound England which was in control of that country. Spanish envoys were finally sent to Basle and Bayonne; an offensive launched by Moncey, who occupied Bilbao and advanced as far as the Ebro, made Godoy more conciliatory, while the Committee, preoccupied with the landing of the émigrés at Quiberon, modified its demands. On 4 Thermidor (July 22), Spain got off with the renunciation of its part of Santo Domingo.

The time had come to settle the question of the country's frontiers if a general peace was to be negotiated. Thugut was not in favor of negotiating, for he had just obtained some subsidies from England, but on May 17, an agreement had established the demarcation line which consecrated the neutrality of North Germany; on July 3, the Reichstag accepted Prussia's good offices to negotiate with France, and on August 28, Hesse-Cassel, without waiting any longer, signed a peace treaty. The princes of South Germany, being restrained only by fear of Austria, would have followed her example unhesitatingly if Prussia had promised them her support. In that case, Austria would have been unable to attack France except across the Alps, thanks to an alliance with the King of Sardinia, and her efforts would have been hopeless; all the more reason why she would have agreed to conclude peace if Belgium had been returned to her. But it was impossible to obtain Prussia's support without giving up the Rhine. Hardenberg kept pressing France to do this, arguing that it did not follow that she would gain nothing: it would be agreed that she should adjust her frontier with Belgium, and that she should keep Trier, part of the Palatinate, and Luxembourg which had capitulated on June 8.

In the absence of Reubell and Sieyès, the Committee had hesitated again, even with regard to Belgium. Questioned in Floréal about the Rhine frontier, Merlin de Thionville replied: "You are putting me to a cruel test. Who can have any definite opinion on that terrifying question?" However, he ended up by advising the Committee to confine itself to annexing Speier, Trier and Luxembourg "as far as the Meuse which would become our limit," thus abandoning the greater part of Belgium. On 3 Prairial (May 22), Merlin de Douai wrote to Barthélemy that since the Convention had not expressed an opinion it remained at liberty to give up the Rhine. But Reubell and Sieyès returned on 4 Prairial and, with Treilhard, formed an unshakable block. The Committee did not commit itself in public, but it rejected Hardenberg's suggestions. True, it tried to coax Thugut by offering him Bavaria and by exchanging Madame Royale for the members of the Convention handed over by Dumouriez in 1793, but the proposals it put forward on 8 Messidor (June 26) allowed no room for hope: in return for Bavaria, it wanted Belgium, and also Lombardy for the King of Sardinia; Poland was to be restored for the benefit of a Prussian prince, and Austria was to join a league against Russia and England. It goes without saying that Thugut refused.

This being so, there was nothing to be done but fight Austria to the bitter end: it was necessary to cross the Rhine and march on Vienna. But the Thermidorians could not manage to agree on this point either. On 15 Prairial Merlin de Douai had left the Committee; on 15 Messidor, it was the turn of Reubell and Sieyès, and Aubry's influence immediately began to grow; hoping that some day or other the party of the former limits would carry the day on the Committee, he did all he could to stop the offensive and even proposed breaking up the Army of the Rhine for the benefit of the other armies. Treilhard succeeded only in getting a decision postponed until the generals had been consulted.

These hesitations cannot be explained simply by the instability of the Executive and the ulterior motives of those Thermidorians who were favorable to the Royalists. Aubry also knew that the country could no longer afford to undertake large-scale operations, and cited the complaints of the generals and the representatives about the appalling destitution of the armies. The Thermidorians were no longer in a position to wage war, and this was the most serious consequence of their policies. Under the pretext of economy, but also out of hostility toward the *sans-culotte* workers and toward State enterprise, they had gradually stopped the manufacture of armaments. In Pluviôse, the Parisian workshops which still remained had been closed; the building of national factories, particularly at Tulle, Saint-Denis, and Saint-Cloud, was abandoned in Germinal. Since Brumaire, the manufacture of saltpeter had slowed down; it had been stopped at Troyes in Frimaire and at Aubusson in Pluviôse; finally, on 17 Germinal (April 6), it ceased to be compulsory and was abandoned completely. On 21 Germinal, the Powder Agency had been reorganized and its personnel reduced. Similarly, the workshops set up by the districts to provide the armies with clothes, equipment and bedding were neglected; then, on 12 Ventôse (March 2), orders were given to suspend purchases and dismiss the workers. Only the requisitioning of "decadal" shoes was retained.

Then again, as the quotas were no longer delivered punctually, the armies were deprived of bread and fodder. The purchases made by the Supplies Commission remained inadequate because of the food shortage. On 5 Germinal (March 25), the ration was reduced from twenty-eight to twenty-four ounces, and the soldier who received a pound could consider himself lucky; on 5 Prairial (May 24), sifting was abolished for flour intended for ration bread; three quarters of it was supposed to be corn, but in fact corn gave place to oats and rye.. As for the army's pay, it was issued irregularly, and in *assignats*. Now, the soldier received only bread, and theoretically, half a pound of meat. On 5 Thermidor (July 23), it was finally decided to promise him two of his ten sous a day in metallic currency, and to grant officers eight francs a month. But finding them was a problem.

The Supplies Commission, known as the "Starvation Commission," was held responsible for the armies' destitution as well as for the hunger riots, and the contractors' campaign to obtain the abolition of the agencies made rapid strides. The government gradually handed over to private enterprise the manufacture of armaments and what remained of the national factories; it increased the number of contracts, particularly as far as food supplies were concerned. The most important contract was placed through the instrumentality of the representative Lefebvre de Nantes who, assisted by an Antwerp trader called Werbrouck, had got in touch in Brussels with the big banking and trading firm directed by Walckiers; they promised to supply Paris and the armies of the North and of the Sambre and Meuse for eighteen months, beginning on 1 Messidor.

Once the agreement had been concluded, they came to an understanding with their fellow countrymen, the Simons brothers, former traders and bankers in Paris whence they had fled at the end of 1793 to settle in Hamburg. The Simons brothers sold them 4,000 lasts (200,000 quintals) of grain, making a profit of over one and a half million livres. An operation on such a vast scale, although it kept the form of a contract for specific quantities, was clearly another step towards the return to those contracts of the *ancien régime* which left the task of supplying the armies to private contractors, in return for a fixed price. This was certainly how Lefebvre saw it:

> In accepting the proposed tender, I see first of all the advantage of ridding the government of the agencies and their peculations; I see the Committees relieved of a host of cares which are wasting their valuable time. Looking further afield, it would not be impossible to set up a similar establishment in the south of France.

The government seems to have anticipated this advice, for it had already placed a contract with a certain Fondreton Company to supply grain to the western armies. Similar developments were taking place in the sphere of transport. On 11 Prairial (May 30), the Transport, Post and Parcels Commission was abolished and its place taken by a Post and Parcels Office; the Internal Navigation Agency remained, but land transport was entrusted to the Army Movements Commission, which used the existing matériel and hired horses from the Lanchère Company. It was thus made clear that in future the State intended to undertake responsibility for military transport only. Even so, on 3 Thermidor (July 21) the latter was entrusted, in the case of the Armies of Italy and of the Alps, to the Michel and Roux Company, which took over the Republic's wagons and undertook to supply, on a contractual basis, the necessary equipment and animals: here the wheel had turned full circle.

In point of fact, the system did not become general as yet, the principal reason probably being that the shortage of food and the instability of prices confronted private enterprise with excessive difficulties. Many contracts were in fact canceled and the contractors did no better than the commissions and their agencies. The representatives with the Army of the Rhine and Moselle reported on 22 Ventôse (March 12) that Cerf Zacharias had failed to supply anything; those with the Army of the Western Pyrenees noted on 22 Messidor (July 10) that the Lanchère Company had kept none of its engagements; on 20 Messidor, the Fondreton Company canceled its contract for the western armies. That is why the Supplies Commission and its agencies continued their operations; for example, they resumed their work for the western armies. Moreover, the contractors did not afford the Treasury as much relief as had been thought: Walckiers and Werbrouk had asked for an advance of one third or one quarter on their contract. Finally, extortions had started immediately; on 4 Thermidor (July 22), the Committee of Public Safety expressed indignation at the fact that Cerf Berr, having been provided with the horses which the Republic had bought abroad for between 580 and 600 livres in metallic currency, proposed to pay only 1,500 livres for them in *assignats* which were not worth more than fifty.

In Year III, therefore, the troops suffered much greater hardship than in Year II, and their plight was the same as that of the civilian population. If the discipline and civic devotion of the armies did not diminish—and the representatives admiringly bore witness to this—it was because the number of soldiers who remained loyal fell to an unprecedented extent: the malcontents deserted *en masse*, as soon as they could do so safely. In Ventôse, out of a theoretical strength of 1,100,000 men, there already remained only 454,000 in fact; 119,000 of these were in France, leaving only 335,000 for operations beyond the frontiers. During the summer, the scale of desertion increased. In Messidor, in the Army of the Alps, it was at the rate of 1,000 to 2,000 men every ten days; a battalion of 800 men, going from Lyons to Grenoble, lost 650 of them. On 10 Thermidor (July 28), Aubry proposed granting an amnesty, but the fugitives incurred no risk by ignoring it.

It should be noted that, in spite of everything, Jourdan and Moncey were able to render the services required of them. If the offensive began late and went badly, that was largely because of Pichegru's treachery. His easy success in Holland had earned him an unjustified reputation which had turned his head; in that country he had contracted luxurious and above all intemperate habits, and his mistress, the wife of Lajolais, his chief of staff, cost him a great deal of money. The agents of the Prince of Condé—especially Fauche-Borel, a Neufchâtel bookseller enrolled by Montgaillard in agreement with Wickham, the English representative in Switzerland—filled his purse every time they saw him, and he took the money shamelessly. The Royalists asked him to deliver Hüningen into their hands and to declare himself against the Convention; he disappointed them, for he was waiting to see how things were going to turn out in Paris, but he gave no reply to the Committee's demands and made no preparations. Thus he delayed the offensive until September, and when the order was given for it to be launched, his army was not in a position to make an effective contribution. It must be granted that the Committee of Year II would not have given him so much rope.

The Thermidorians were therefore incapable of bringing the war to an end, either by offering a peace without conquests or by forcing Austria to extremities with a merciless offensive. Both abroad and at home, far from directing events, they let things drift. All the same, Thugut, busy watching Prussia and settling the Polish affair, could not cause them any serious anxiety. This was precisely the moment the English chose to stage the landing which would have been so effective in 1793, at the time of the Vendeans' victories. In April 1795, Puisaye had finally won approval for his plans from Windham, Pitt's colleague. However, the British ministers did not commit themselves very far: they provided money and a naval squadron, but not a single man. Puisaye formed an army of émigrés who were equipped, it is true, with British uniforms; he hoped to recruit 12,000 men, but as the number of volunteers fell short of this, he filled the gap with French prisoners who agreed to enlist in order to escape from the hulks into which they were crowded; two divisions were formed in this way under the command of d'Hervilly and Sombreuil. The émigrés expected the south of France to rise in revolt, and Condé to enter Alsace and Franche-Comté, thanks to Pichegru, but they did not wait for this support to become apparent because they cherished illusions about the extent of the revolt which the Chouans and the Vendeans had been asked to foment. At the beginning of May, Puisaye, commander-in-chief of the expedition, had informed the Comte de Sils, his principal confederate in the Morbihan, who summoned the Royalist leaders to a meeting at Grand-champ on 1 Prairial (May 20). Two days later, a Royalist courier was arrested at Ploermel, and his dispatches acquainted the Committee of Public Safety with what was afoot: Cormatin was arrested on the fifth and, the troops having started moving, de Sils was killed on the eighth. Cadoudal took his place, but as Hoche had advanced in force towards the south coast of Brittany, the Chouans were able to carry out only a few operations and the greater part of the population did not budge. As for the Vendean leaders, annoyed that the expedition was not intended for them, they waited for it to arrive before taking up arms. The Convention sent three representatives to the west; on 30 Prairial (June 18), it attached a military commission to each army and pronounced sentence of death on any rebel found bearing arms.

From the captured dispatches Hoche knew approximately where the landing was due to take place; from the conversation of the Royalists in Paris, the Committee knew that it was imminent. Admiral Villaret was ordered to bar the way to the invasion fleet, but Bridport defeated him and forced him to take refuge at Lorient on 5 Messidor (June 23). The same day, an English frigate landed Tinténiac and du Bois-Berthelot, who gathered together a certain number of peasants—14,000, it is said—provided them with red coats, and, at their head, seized control of the coast near the Quiberon peninsula. D'Hervilly's division was then able to land on the ninth (June 27).

A strange conflict had just broken out between its commander and Puisaye, for d'Hervilly had displayed a document appointing him commander-in-chief. Puisaye, it is true, had told Windham that if the landing proved impossible, he would nonetheless go ashore with a few officers to encourage the Chouans, whereupon the English minister had remarked that, while waiting to rejoin their leader, the troops ought to be directed by another general whom Puisaye could appoint his second-in-command. But the letter of appointment delivered to d'Hervilly would appear to have contained no qualification, and seemed to dispossess Puisaye. It is difficult to imagine that Windham would have been guilty of such ineptitude, and some historians, instead of blaming the negligence of his subordinates, have preferred to suggest that among the latter the Absolutists of the Paris agency had found an accomplice to thwart the Constitutionalist Puisaye; in support of this thesis, they cite the Abbé Brottier's letters to d'Hervilly, addressing him as commander-in-chief and putting him on guard against his rival, as well as to the leaders of the Chouans in the Morbihan, warning them not to take up arms except on the orders of the Council of Princes. Whatever the truth of the matter, the dispute paralyzed the command of the expedition. A few days went by before d'Hervilly agreed to take the offensive; during the night of 14-15 Messidor (July 2-3), Fort Penthièvre, which commanded the entrance to the peninsula, was finally captured; the Chouans had already taken Auray and a few villages to make the approaches secure. However, d'Hervilly and his forces went no farther, and it was decided that they should wait for Sombreuil, who, with his division, did not leave England until the twenty-first (July 9).

Hoche thus had time to concentrate his troops. In order to avoid engaging them piecemeal, he had chosen Hennebont as a rallying point. Once he was ready, he recaptured Auray from the Chouans and pushed them back on to the peninsula, where they quarreled with the émigrés who, full of contempt for these peasants, had failed to give them any support. In a single week, Hoche established a solid line of trenches which turned the peninsula into a mousetrap, handed over the command to Lemoine and went off to the rear to speed up the arrival of reinforcements.

Thoroughly alarmed, the Royalists attempted a breakout on 19 Messidor (July 7), but suffered a costly defeat. In order to take the Republicans in the rear, they then sent some detachments of Chouans to Pont-Aven, Pouldu, Carnac and Sarzeau. The first three detachments scattered or failed to achieve anything; the émigrés counted above all on the fourth, which had been placed under the command of Tinténiac and Cadoudal, but after landing on the twenty-third, it made northwards, creating yet another mystery.

From Jersey, an attack was supposed to be launched on Saint-Malo during the night of 21-22 Messidor; as it happened, it was abandoned because the men who were to deliver the city into the émigrés' hands were arrested in time; but Boisguy, in Ile-et-Vilaine, had not budged, waiting, it is thought, for this attack, and it may have been to join him and the expeditionary corps that Tinténiac went north. However, pending the intervention of this new army, the émigrés on Quiberon would have been left to their fate, and it is difficult to believe that this was the mission with which they had entrusted Tinténiac; his attitude, like that of Boisguy, has therefore been attributed to the activities of the Paris agency. In the absence of the planned diversions, the attack made by the émigrés, supported by Sombreuil, ended on 28 Messidor (July 16) in a fresh reverse; d'Hervilly was mortally wounded. As for Tinténiac, he was defeated and killed on the 30th. Cadoudal took over the command and led his men as far as the sea: they scattered at the news of the final disaster.

At the news of the encounter of the twenty-eighth, Hoche had hurriedly returned. Tallien and Blad, sent along on the thirteenth by the Convention, joined him. The decisive attack was fixed for the night of 2-3 Thermidor (July 20-21). The columns on the left and in the center, hampered by a storm, spotted and bombarded, were hesitating when, in the light of dawn, they saw the tricolor flag flying on Fort Penthièvre: a small band of men, keeping to the west coast, had entered the fort, thanks to the defection of the soldiers recruited in the English jails. The émigrés, taken by surprise, were unable to restore the battle and fell back to the tip of the peninsula in appalling confusion. Puisaye had regained the English squadron, and some of the émigrés were able to follow his example. The others laid down their arms with Sombreuil. To begin with, nobody said anything about a formal capitulation, which would have guaranteed that the émigrés' lives would be spared, and Sombreuil himself did not avail himself of this opportunity; but in front of one of the military commissions, some of the prisoners invoked it. Hoche and Blad flatly denied that any such agreement had been concluded, although it is possible that the accused believed that it existed when they saw their leader conversing with Hoche and the representatives, and even that some officers and men made reassuring remarks to them.

The exact number of the prisoners is not known; there were about a thousand émigrés, between three and four thousand Chouans, and three thousand Republicans enrolled in England. Many of them escaped. The rest were tried by twenty military commissions set up by Blad. Tallien, who had returned to Paris, did nothing to recommend clemency and the Convention remained silent. Two thousand nine hundred and eighteen Republicans and twelve hundred Chouans were acquitted. But the decree of 23 Brumaire was applied to the émigrés and 748 were shot. The law was clear, and Blad, in the midst of rebel country, was no more inclined than was the army to spare the Coalition's auxiliaries, captured wearing British uniforms, especially as the Vendean insurrection had begun again and Charette had inaugurated it by wiping out a guard-post in a surprise attack and putting to death hundreds of prisoners afterwards. For a moment he had grounds for hoping that the English were at last going to come to his aid. On September 30, Warren appeared off the coast and captured the island of Yeu, where he landed the Comte d'Artois with a few troops. But the Prince was in no hurry to join the Vendean leaders, who were already hard pressed; he secretly asked the British government to recall the expedition, and finally the island of Yeu was evacuated without any attempt being made to reach the mainland. As for Stofflet, he only resumed operations at the end of January 1796.

The pitiful adventure of the émigrés, ill-conceived and ill-conducted, raised the hatred which England inspired in France to fever-pitch. Moreover, the danger had re-awakened the revolutionary spirit: Hoche's victory finally consolidated the Republic.

CHAPTER NINE

The Constitution of Year III

The émigrés' enterprise had deeply moved public opinion; the Royalists, full of hope, lost no opportunity of exciting it still further. They spread a rumor that distributions of food were going to be suspended in Paris, that there was going to be a new levy of men, and that, as Bailleul reported on 25 Messidor (July 30), "the Committees of Public Safety and of General Security had met to decide whether to re-establish the system of the Terror and that only two voices had been raised in opposition." In their papers, as the Committee of General Security observed on 21 Thermidor (August 8), every page contained "the most revolting satires on the government's activities, cries of sedition, and expressions of hate for the Republic."

The Republicans had no such dark designs, but it was true that the danger they had undergone had reawakened the revolutionary spirit in them. On 26 Messidor, the anniversary of the taking of the Bastille was celebrated by great pomp in the Convention, where the National Institute of Music performed the *Marseillaise*. "It is impossible," said the *Moniteur*, "to describe the effect produced by those unexpected strains which we had forgotten for some time past"; it incidentally expressed regret that the *Réveil du peuple* had not been played too, and this omission was indeed characteristic. In the midst of general enthusiasm, Debry got a decree passed that the *Marseillaise* should be played every day at the changing of the guard.

The Thermidorians did not show an exclusive spirit and appealed to all those who had co-operated in the Revolution. "Republicans, Anglomaniacs of '89, Constitutionalists of '91," cried Doulcet on 13 Messidor (July 1), "the same fate awaits you, the same flag must unite you; march all together to exterminate executioners who have no other desire but that of vengeance." But if the Constitutional Monarchists dreaded the victory of the émigrés, they were reluctant to declare against them. It was the *sans-culottes* who responded to the cry of alarm; it would have been easy for them to protest that in 1793, the moderates, rather than join with them to save the nation and the Republic, had preferred to unleash civil war at the risk of losing both; they forgot their grievances as soon as it was a question of fighting the aristocrats.

At the Palais Égalité and on the boulevards, the workers from the suburbs reappeared and made common cause

with the soldiers, now so numerous in Paris, against the
fops. "Attacks are being made on the green cravats and
the black collars," announced the *Courrier républicain* on
8 Messidor (June 26). Duval has said something of this
"war of the black collars":

> After the shouts came oaths; after the oaths came blows.
> They hit us, they struck us, they threw mud in our faces
> and at our poor collars; then they set to work with scissors
> and it was our hair's turn to suffer. They beat up those of us
> who were on our own and more than one of us was obliged
> to receive baptism by immersion in the Palais Royal foun-
> tain.

After the Convention had paid honor to the *Marseillaise*,
a new quarrel arose and spread all over France. A report
by Delaunay sums it up as follows: "The hymn to liberty,
it is said, accompanied the victims of the bloodthirsty
Robespierre to the scaffold, and the Convention wants
to revive the Terror. The hymn of the *Réveil du peuple* fills
the terrorists with alarm: it alone must be sung." In the
evening of the twenty-sixth, the "young men" imposed
the latter at the Opéra; on the twenty-eighth, at the Café
de Chartres, they loudly declared that "if the Convention
decreed a levy, they would rather let their ears be cut off
than join the colors"; on the thirtieth, their gangs laid siege
to the Committee of General Security to obtain the release of two actors arrested the day before, during the
disturbances in the theatres, and gave a thrashing to
Sergeant-Major Devaux, who had covered himself with
glory at Fleurus. But the time had passed when the government treated them as auxiliaries; Fréron and above all
Tallien, who was heaped with insults as the man responsible for the slaughter at Quiberon, had become Republi-

cans again. The police closed the Café de Chartres, made raids on the boulevards, and surrounded the theatres and ballrooms to look for absentees and deserters among the fops. The Committees had a few journalists arrested, and, by restoring subsidies, reconstituted a Republican press. The *Moniteur* was joined in Messidor by Louvet's *Sentinelle*, and Lemaire's *Journal du Bonhomme Richard*; in Fructidor, Réal's gazette became *Le Journal des patriotes de 89*, and Poultier, a former monk and member of the Convention, founded *L'Ami des lois*.

It might therefore have been thought that, in the Convention, the division which had appeared once more, after Prairial, between the Center and the Right, would become wider. Nothing of the sort happened. The Constitutional Monarchists inveighed against Hoche and Tallien in the corridors and salons, but could not think of anything to do for the moment but collaborate in the constitutional task and speed up the elections, from which they hoped for great things. For their part, the Thermidorians of the Center needed the Right to complete their work: they accordingly made concessions. On 8 Messidor (June 26), the Committee of General Security had recalled that citizens were free to dress as they pleased; on the twenty-eighth (July 16), it forbade the singing on the stage of any song which did not form part of the play or opera being performed; at the celebration of the anniversaries of the ninth of Thermidor and the tenth of August, the *Réveil du peuple* was sung at the same time as the *Marseillaise*. The Center was not sorry to exclude from the coming election those deputies who were denounced as terrorists. It was in vain that Dubois-Crancé, who had returned to the Left, demanded that the decree of 21 Brumaire should be respected: on 21 and 22 Thermidor (August 8 and 9), the arrest of ten more Montagnards was decreed, among them Fouché himself. It was more difficult to reach agreement about the imprisoned patriots, a few of whom were released by the Committee of General Security every day, to the fury of the Sections. On 3 Thermidor (July 21), the Committees had proposed a compromise and offered to send them before the indictment juries, except in Paris where their case would be submitted to a commission chosen by the Convention. Bentabole and Berlier obtained a decision, on the sixth, that this commission would have full powers throughout France. But the Right reacted strongly. "The truth must out," declared Bailleul; "this means impunity for the guilty." The Sections spoke up in support. The Committees gave way, and on the nineteenth (August 6), the decree of the sixth was revoked. It was only on 11 Fructidor (August 28) that agreement was reached: all those who had been arrested without a warrant were sent before a police officer who would decide, in conformity with the Penal Code, whether there were grounds for prosecution. In point of fact, the Committee of General Security went on releasing prisoners, and on the second *jour complémentaire* (September 18), the Convention itself appreciably reduced the scope of its decree by deciding that the persons arrested on the orders of its Committees or of the representatives could not be committed for trial except by a decree of the former. In public, the reactionaries accused it of having contrived to save the terrorists, and this accusation played a considerable part on the thirteenth of Vendémiaire. A good many *sans-*

culottes nonetheless found themselves in prison at the time of the plebiscite and the elections, the decree of 11 Fructidor having been too late to obtain their release.

These discussions had not prevented the Thermidorians of all shades of opinion from passing the Constitution of Year III, which was substituted for that of 1793, now tacitly considered as canceled, like the plebiscite which had sanctioned it. The commission of eleven, appointed on 29 Germinal (April 18) had worked on it for two months. It included some sincere Republicans such as Thibaudeau, La Revellière, Louvet, Berlier, Daunou and Baudin des Ardennes, and a few deputies whom Thibaudeau regarded as Monarchists—Boissy d'Anglas, Lanjuinais and Lesage d'Eure-et-Loir—but who were postponing their hopes until a later date. Boissy was elected chairman and presented the project on 5 Messidor (June 23). The debate, in two readings, took two months, and the final vote was taken on 5 Fructidor (August 22).

In the preparation of this Constitution, two principles guided both the Thermidorian Republicans and the Constitutional Monarchists: barring the way to democracy and preventing the advent of a dictatorship of any description. They returned to the principles of the Constituent Assembly, interpreting them as the latter had done at the time of the revision of 1791, while retouching its work in the light of recent experience and referring to the lower classes in a tone of suspicion and contempt which it had never used. If they thought fit to formulate a Declaration of Rights, they were careful to eliminate from it the essential article: "Men are born and remain free and equal in rights." To those who proposed restoring it, Mailhe and Lanjuinais replied on 26 Thermidor (August 13) that

it was ambiguous and therefore dangerous: men were no
doubt equal in rights, but not in ability or in property
either; in adopting this article, the Constituent Assembly
had not realized that it was banning in advance the property
qualification for suffrage. "Civil equality," Boissy had said,
"is all a reasonable man can demand." The following
definition was therefore adopted: "Equality consists in the
fact that the law is the same for all." This was indeed what
the Constituent Assembly had meant to say; thus defined,
equality became a sort of attribute of liberty which it confined itself to insuring for everybody. The State had no
other function but to guarantee that liberty by maintaining
order, which in practice amounted to allowing one group of
citizens to subjugate the rest by means of their ability and
above all by means of their wealth. This was also the view
of the Thermidorians and they consequently struck out the
articles in the Declaration of 1793 which had expressed a
different idea of the State, that of a social democracy
which intervenes to restore, for the benefit of the poor, the
equilibrium destroyed by money. The article to the effect
that "the aim of society is the common happiness" aroused
Lanjuinais' sarcasm; and when the right to work was
brought up, Thibault exclaimed: "They will come and ask
you for bread again!" In the sphere of politics, universal
suffrage disappeared, without finding any defenders other
than Paine, Lanthenas and the little-known Souhait. The
referendum suffered the same fate; the new regime was
purely representative, although the Declaration had stated
that "the law is the general will expressed by the majority
of the citizens or by the majority of their representatives."
The right to insurrection naturally went the same way.
Freedom of the press was retained but the Legislature was

authorized to suspend it for a period of one year. The right of public meeting was restored, but with all the restrictions which had been imposed on the Jacobin clubs before their suppression. Economic freedom on the other hand was, needless to say, fully consecrated. Finally, it was thought fit to add to the declaration of the citizen's rights a declaration of his duties which was to serve as a catechism for the decadal religion, and which preached, to citizens deprived of the right to vote, obedience to laws that they had not made.

In some respects, the Convention showed itself more democratic than the Constituent Assembly: the Constitution of Year III was submitted to popular ratification, and, as it would have taken time to draw up a list of voting and tax-paying citizens, or *citoyens actifs,* universal suffrage was maintained for the plebiscite as well as for the first election. The electoral qualification was fixed in a more liberal way than in 1791: all Frenchmen over twenty-one years old, and in residence for one year, became *citoyens actifs* if they paid any sort of tax, even a voluntary contribution. In the future, however, the suffrage was to sustain a restriction which was extremely severe for the times: as of Year XII, the *citoyen actif* would have to be able to read and write; it is true that in compensation it was stipulated that he should be engaged in a manual occupation, but this tribute to Rousseau could only be a pure formality. Besides, in Year III, the provisional retention of universal suffrage was not as important as it might appear, because the election of deputies took place in two stages and a solid barrier was raised between the *citoyens actifs* and the electors. The former met in a primary assembly at the seat of a canton to choose the latter from among Frenchmen over twenty-five years old, who were the owners of a property yielding a revenue equal to the value of 200 days of work in places of 6,000 inhabitants or more, and tenants anywhere else of a house with a rent equal to 150 days or of a country property with a farm rent of 200. The electors traveled at their own expense to the electoral assembly to appoint the deputies. The Commission had required the latter to be landowners and had stipulated that, in order to qualify for the Legislature, they should have passed by way of the lower elected positions. The Convention set aside these two articles: no qualification was therefore imposed on the representatives of the people, but simply an age requirement.

In the organization of the public powers, the separation of powers was the guiding principle, since the Commission wanted to avoid a dictatorship, even that of an assembly. As the aristocracy seemed to have been finally eliminated, there was no longer any objection to the two-chamber system: the legislative power was divided between the 250 Ancients, who had to be over forty and either married men or widowers, and the Five Hundred, who had to be at least thirty. What is more, one third of each house had to retire and be replaced every year. The Five Hundred had the initiative and passed resolutions which the Ancients could turn into laws. As a precaution against popular riots, the latter had the right to move the seat of the assemblies and the government outside Paris. As a precaution against the army, a constitutional belt, into which it could not penetrate without permission, surrounded the capital. As for the executive power, the Commission refused to entrust it to a President of the Republic, who might have attempted to gain personal power, and to allow him to be chosen by the people—who, Louvet had said, according to Thibaudeau, would have been perfectly capable of picking a Bourbon. It was conferred on a Directory of five members, appointed by the Ancients from a list of ten candidates nominated by the Five Hundred; one of the five was to retire and be replaced every year. According to Boissy, it was to act as a continuation of the Committee of Public Safety: "It will have the same range of power." In place of the executive commissions, six ministers were subordinated to it whom it chose and dismissed at will, and who were merely its agents. Like the Committee, it had no authority over the Treasury, which was entrusted to six commissioners elected under the same conditions as the Directors; what is more, it was not allowed the initiative in proposing laws, and it was simply permitted to give the councils advice in the form of *messages*. Nor did it have the authority over departmental administration which the revolutionary government had given the Committees and the representatives on mission and which had been retained for the Legislative Committee. The decentralization carried out by the Constituent Assembly was restored, though not without considerable modifications; for reasons of economy, the department no longer had a general council or a directory, but simply a "central administration" of five members chosen by the electoral assembly; the district was abolished because of the part it had played in Year II and in order to reduce the influence of the towns on the country areas. The result was that the district courts likewise disappeared, and only one civil court remained in each department. "Municipal administrations" were set up which were directly subordinate to the departmental administration. However, as it had been impossible to recruit competent and educated personnel in the villages, they were grouped together with the small towns of fewer than 5,000 inhabitants to form a single municipality for each canton, the *citoyens actifs* of each commune appointing an agent and an assistant who, together with the agents and assistants of the other communes, formed the municipal administration in the chief town. Since the agent was the executor in his commune of decisions adopted in an assembly over which its electors could exercise no supervision, and was himself supervised only at a great distance by the departmental administration, he became a sort of potentate who could do as he pleased. The big towns, on the contrary, lost their autonomy; Paris remained under the control of government officials, as she had been since Thermidor; the other big towns were divided into areas whose municipalities were linked only by a central office. Here, therefore, the State saw its power indirectly increased, since it no longer had any reason to fear either the rivalry of the Commune of Paris or the secession of Lyons, Marseilles and Bordeaux. Moreover, the Directory was granted rather more power over the departmental authorities than the Constituent Assembly had conferred on the King. It was authorized to suspend them and change their personnel until the following elections which were annual, and above all, commissioners chosen by the Directory were attached to the central administration of each department and to the municipal administrations. These officials rendered important technical services; they were comparatively stable in comparison with the elected officials, who were liable to be changed frequently, and became the real regional officials, so that they were able to prepare and co-ordinate the work of the assemblies. Legally, they could only demand the enforcement of the law, and, having been chosen in the region, could not always escape from local influence. The departmental commissioner, in fact, was more like the Secretary-General of the Consulate than the Prefect, whose authority he lacked, so that the departmental regime was closer to that of the Constituent Assembly than to that of Year II or of the Consulate. But as the commissioner often exceeded his powers, he nonetheless served in practice as a link between these last two systems.

Taken by itself, outside the context of time and place, it may be that this Constitution of Year III deserves the praise which has often been given it. Destined for a country whose revolution, more social than political in nature, was not complete, a country which had to wage a war that showed no sign of coming to an end, without money, without currency and in the midst of a grave food shortage, it was a sort of wager, since everything about it was arranged so that legislation should be as slow as possible and, above all, so that the Executive should remain weak and lifeless. Yet if Sieyès had had his way, the central power would have been weaker still. The account he gave on 2 Thermidor (July 20) of his ideas on the Constitution was the most interesting episode in the commission's discussions. Against the social idea of the rights of man, which can only acquire reality through the protection of the State and *ipso facto* accept the restriction applied by the State, to the degree implied by its very existence, Sieyès set the natural rights prior to the State and showed that the essential object of the Constitution was on the contrary to limit the latter's power to the strict minimum. In very strong terms, he therefore refused to grant the general will the omnipotence which Rousseau had attributed to it; in other words, he repudiated the sovereignty of the people which was simply a transposition of royal absolutism and, as a result, challenged the representatives' "unlimited powers," which he described as "a political monstrosity." He said:

> When a political association is formed, the members do not pool all the rights which each individual brings to that society, or the power of the entire mass of individuals. They pool, under the name of public or political power, the least they can, and only what is necessary to preserve the rights and duties of each individual. This portion of power is a long way from resembling the exaggerated notions with which some people have been pleased to invest what they call sovereignty: and note well that it is the sovereignty of the people that I am talking about, for if any sovereignty exists, that is it. This word makes such a profound impression on the imagination only because the French mind, still full of monarchical superstition, has made a point of endowing it with all the heritage of pompous attributes and absolute powers that have lent glory to the usurped sovereignties.

In order to prevent the State, regarded as a sort of public enemy, from encroaching on the rights of the individual, Sieyès too resorted to the separation of powers, but in this respect the Thermidorians' work struck him as superficial; in his eyes the division of the legislative power between two chambers was totally insufficient to destroy its omnipotence. He proposed reserving the initiative for the government, considered on this account as a *jurie de proposition*, entrusting a tribunate with the task of examining projects and a legislature with that of passing them, and finally setting up a *jurie constitutionnaire* to which one of the councils, the minority of one of them, or any citizen, could denounce the promulgated law, as well as electoral operations, judgments of the appeal court and acts of the executive and its officials, as being inimical to the Constitution.

This *jurie constitutionnaire* was no doubt simply an imitation of the Supreme Court of the United States. But this was not the sum total of its powers. Every ten years, it would be entitled to take the initiative in revising the law of the land, and the primary assemblies, on presentation of its proposals, could then confer upon the Legislature constituent authority to accept or reject those proposals, but without being able to modify them. Finally, every year, one tenth of its members, drawn by lot, would form a *jurie d'équité* which the courts could ask for judgments, on the plea that it was impossible for them to pass judgment, either because the law was silent, or because to do so would have been "contrary to their conscience." As for the government, once a law had been passed, it became a *jurie d'exécution* and appointed the ministers, each of whom was to be the sole master of his sphere of activity, so that, with the central power broken up in this way, unity of action would be nothing but a myth.

The basic thesis could only appeal to the Thermidorians, and the Commission of Eleven gave its support to Sieyès' proposals; La Revellière defended them before the Convention. Berlier and Eschassériaux also approved the idea of a *jurie constitutionnaire*, but they did not fail to see that the system, if adopted in its entirety, would end up in practice by paralyzing the State and lead to anarchical individualism; Berlier did not agree with the possibility of an appeal by the minority of the representatives, while Eschassériaux rejected the *jurie d'équité*. Louvet and Thibaudeau attacked the *jurie constitutionnaire* itself, and, together with Lesage, maintained that the two-chamber system provided all the safeguards it was reasonable to expect. They carried the Assembly with them and on 25 Thermidor (August 12),

Sieyès' project was unanimously rejected. Deeply hurt, Sieyès adopted, right from the start, an attitude of opposition to the Directory, and in Year VII brought about its downfall. Several elements of his plan were then incorporated in the Constitution of Year VIII, with the lamentable result that they helped Bonaparte in his rise to power; the *jurie constitutionnaire* became that Conservatory Senate which was the tool of despotism and conserved nothing at all. More moderate and realistic in her views, Madame de Staël, in her *Réflexions sur la paix intérieure*, had suggested reinforcing the authority of the Ancients and giving the Executive a limited right of veto.

Once the Constitution had been approved, the Thermidorians tried to rally the Constitutional Monarchists and the Democrats to its support. Thus Réal, on 7 Fructidor (August 24), said: "Patriots of '89, Constitutional Monarchists, Jacobins; moderates, *exagérés*, democrats, Republicans; all of you, in fact, who have made the Revolution or allowed it to be made, open your eyes: nothing remains for you but liberty or death." And Louvet, on the fourth, declared: "Each of the parties that have divided France can recognize in the Constitution all the wisest things it has called for." They had no cause to feel anxious about the plebiscite which was to ratify their work. The Feuillants had collaborated in it; the Absolutists saw in it the advantage of getting rid of the Convention; as for the *sans-culottes*, with social democracy set aside, instinct advised them to keep the future open to it by maintaining at least the form of a Republic. But once the plebiscite was over, the elections would have to follow and the situation would be entirely different. There was no reason to be afraid of the Jacobins: their leaders were in prison and on 5 Fructidor (August 22) those deputies who had been indicted or whose arrest had been decreed were declared ineligible. The danger came from the Royalists, for, if they had accepted the Constitution, it was because they felt certain of obtaining a majority; in that case the Republic would be called in question once more and the Revolution itself threatened sooner or later.

CHAPTER TEN

The Thirteenth
of Vendémiaire, Year IV

That the elections were bound to prove fatal to most of
the members of the Convention went without saying. The
nation did not want to return to the *ancien régime* and had
no interest in Louis XVIII; the enemies of the Convention
kept denying that they were Royalists—"Royalism," the
Montmartre Section had said on 11 Thermidor (July 29),
"is a word the terrorists are always using in order to dis-
courage the Republicans who have defended you"—and
they took even greater care not to talk about the tithe,
feudal privileges and the property of the clergy. But the
French people had suffered a great deal and were suffering

more every day; the counterrevolutionaries played on their bitterness at the sacrifices which the Convention had imposed on them, conjured up the specter of the Terror, and promised peace and prosperity. Even if these arguments had failed, no majority could possibly have obtained forgiveness for the prevailing inflation and famine.

There was still practically no course open to the Convention but a massive issue of *assignats*; on 1 Brumaire, the total number in existence would be 22,800,000,000, of which about twenty billion were in circulation. During the course of the summer, the catastrophic consequences of inflation had begun to appear. Since everybody was trying to get rid of the paper money whose value was decreasing from day to day, speculation had reached fever pitch, not only in the vicinity of the Stock Exchange and the Palais Égalité, which was generally known as the Black Forest, but all over Paris, which Mallet du Pan said had become a city of second-hand dealers, and all over France. Prices rose hour by hour and were now ahead of the issue of currency. Since it was impossible to make any plans for the future, the life of business undertakings was threatened: in Fructidor for example, the mines at Littry, in the Calvados, closed down. At Nantes, in Brumaire, Madame Hummel, thoroughly disheartened, would put away her account book, for it had become useless to try to keep household accounts. The social structure of the country was shaken to the foundations, with rentiers, officials and all creditors heading for ruin, while farmers, tenants and debtors liquidated their debts at practically no cost to themselves, and speculators, finding themselves suddenly rich, flaunted scandalous luxury. As for the workers, they were incapable of obtaining wage increases to keep step with the increase in prices which were rising too fast. In Paris, in Thermidor, butter cost eighteen francs a pound and meat eight francs; in Vendémiaire, they cost thirty francs and twenty francs respectively; in the course of that month, the price of a load of wood rose from 500 francs to 800; a pair of shoes cost between 200 and 250 francs. For the great majority of people, these prices were prohibitive. On 12 Thermidor (July 30), Bergoeing had got the Convention to ask the Committees for a plan to "establish uniform food prices based on a proportional scale and reconcilable with the necessary freedom of trade"; but they did not waste their time trying to square this circle, and when, on 3 Brumaire, Year IV (October 25, 1795), Roux proposed returning to the *maximum*, nobody paid any attention.

The peasants no longer brought anything to market, and the towns, which now bought all their food direct from farms or abroad, gradually gave up providing bread for everybody, and looked after nobody but the poor; in other words they simply returned to a system of public assistance, as at Bergues in Messidor, and at Verdun, where in Thermidor the communal bakery was closed down. In other places, the population was divided into classes which were charged different prices for bread; at Dunkirk, in Floréal, three classes were established which paid respectively forty-five, thirty and fifteen sous for a pound loaf, while foreigners were charged ten livres. But these innovations led to constant disturbances: there was a riot at Dunkirk in Thermidor, and at Chartres, on the first *jour complémentaire* (September 17), the representative Tellier, forced by the rioters to fix the price of bread at three sous, committed suicide out of despair. The harvest produced a slight improvement in the situation, but it was not uniformly good, on account of a cold, rainy summer. Consequently the Thermidorian authorities, under the pressure of circumstances, decided to imitate their predecessors and call for a temporary return to controls. The Convention resigned itself to this step. The law of 4 Thermidor (July 22) restored compulsory marketing, except for the benefit of non-harvesters in the country, and limited the individual's purchases for his own consumption until the harvest of Year IV, at the rate of four quintals a head. On 1 Fructidor (August 18), the Committee of Public Safety once again authorized the districts to levy requisitions in order to supply their markets, and once again National Guards were sent out into the country and billeted on recalcitrant farmers. Finally, on 7 Vendémiaire, Year IV (September 29, 1795), a new law on the grain trade laid down, often in fresh detail, the arrangements which had been tried since 1793, with the exception of a fixed price. But the enforcement of the law remained entirely in the hands of the local authorities.

The Parisian population remained in a privileged position, since the government continued to provide it with bread at three sous, while it cost sixteen francs on the open market in Messidor and Thermidor; but it received only a quarter of a pound a head, with a little rice, until the end of Messidor; at the beginning of Thermidor, the ration was generally half a pound, and in Fructidor three-quarters of a pound, which was still very little. As for other foodstuffs, a decree of 27 Thermidor (August 14) granted government officials, rentiers and workers a monthly allowance of four pounds of cod and salt meat, one pound of sugar, one pound of soap and half a pound of oil; for the first time, citizens paying over 150 livres in taxes were excluded, and the others were divided into four classes, the third receiving a quarter less than the fourth, and so on. Even taking into account these allowances, which incidentally it is difficult to estimate with any accuracy, Mr. Harris has calculated that the cost-of-living index, starting at 100 in 1790, nonetheless rose for the Parisian to 2,180 in July, 3,100 in September and 5,340 in November.

The rich themselves found it difficult to obtain food, and a hostess inviting her friends to dinner found herself obliged to ask them to bring their own bread. From Brussels on 14 Prairial (June 2) Lefebvre de Nantes wrote to Merlin de Douai: "I have just posted off a double ration of bread to you." With their thirty-six livres a day, those representatives who did not speculate like Tallien and Fouché were as hard up as the common people; but the latter refused to believe this, and the fops, talking about white bread, used to say: "That's deputy's bread; not everybody can have it." It must be admitted that the members of the Convention obtained a few privileges for themselves; the decree of 27 Thermidor on food allowances granted them twenty-five pounds of cod and salt meat, twelve of sugar, twelve of soap and twenty-five of candles. The most favored were the members of the Committees, and La Revellière has left us an amusing picture of the meetings of the Committee of Public Safety at the end of Year III. Cambacérès, he says, used to arrive about ten o'clock. "The first thing he did was to have a good *pot-au-feu* prepared, and to have some excellent bread and excellent wine put on the table—three things which could scarcely be obtained anywhere else in Paris." His col-

leagues turned up one after another between noon and two
o'clock, and, on being told as usual that there was nothing new,

> visited the *pot-au-feu*, took some broth, and pulled the piece
> of beef out of the stockpot to help themselves to a slice,
> which they ate with some good white bread and washed
> down with an excellent burgundy; then the quivering piece
> of beef would be put back into the stockpot until successive
> cuts had reminded the last comers of the truth of the prov-
> erb, *tarde venientibus ossa*.

It was impossible for these feasts not to be known about
outside, and even more impossible for them not to be
transformed into Rabelaisian banquets to which all the
representatives were invited. Similarly the frauds and speculations of a minority were prejudicial to all, and it was in
vain that the Assembly tried to vindicate the honest deputies by passing a decree, after the thirteenth of Vendémiaire, that every member of the Convention should produce an account of the changes in his fortune since 1789.
The police report on the holiday of the tenth of August,
which was celebrated "in a state of apathy," tells us of
some of the remarks made by members of the public: "The
representatives are celebrating today; the Revolution benefits nobody but them"; and "Public opinion is still very
critical of the representatives who have squandered the
nation's wealth." Some people also said "that they would
rather be under Robespierre's regime; that at that time the
Convention looked after the unfortunate; today, they eat,
drink and enrich themselves at the people's expense."

Conscious of their enormous unpopularity, the Thermidorians, after passing the Constitution, therefore found
themselves faced with the same problem as the Monta-

gnards in 1793. The latter had sidestepped the danger of elections by extending the powers of the Convention until the end of hostilities—an action which, in the midst of civil and foreign war, was easy to justify. As they had repudiated this expedient, the Thermidorians, obliged to institute elections, looked for another device which would at least insure the outgoing members of a majority of seats in the new legislative assembly. The latter was to be renewed one-third at a time to avoid sudden changes in the majority; it was therefore agreed, for the same reason, that the Convention, likewise consisting of 750 members, should bequeath two-thirds of its strength to the new assembly. This was what Baudin explained on behalf of the Commission of Eleven, incidentally without disguising the real motives behind the proposal: "Into what hands is the sacred trust of the Constitution to be placed? . . . In any case we shall be accused of crime or complicity."

But how were the two-thirds going to be chosen? Sieyès, in his project for *jurie constitutionnaire,* had indirectly solved the problem. The jury, renewable one-third at a time by means of co-optation, was to be appointed for the first time by the Convention from among the members of the first three revolutionary assemblies, an arrangement of which the principle at least would be one of the cornerstones of the Constitution of Year VIII. Baudin therefore proposed that the Convention should itself name the outgoing third, but ruled out a ballot on the pretext that it would recall the Jacobin purges. He counted on a sufficient number of resignations; if there were not enough of these, the number would be made up by drawing lots; if the contrary were the case, a jury of nine deputies would choose from among the representatives tendering their resignation those who should be set at liberty. This complicated scheme aroused a certain amount of suspicion, especially as the jury was authorized to consult whatever documents it needed in the archives, and because the plan struck off the active list of deputies, and consequently classified them as outgoing members, those who had been charged or placed under arrest—an obvious attempt to eliminate the deputies of the Left. Tallien and Chénier protested. The next day, 3 Fructidor, Bailleul accordingly proposed that the outgoing members should be selected by ballot; for the Left, the result risked being the same; as for drawing lots, it seems that nobody was in favor of that method, which is understandable. The Right was therefore in a strong position: it wanted the choice of the two-thirds to be left to the electoral assemblies, feeling sure that these would eliminate the Montagnards, as Bailleul bluntly pointed out. The majority of the Thermidorians of the Center, also wanting to get rid of the Montagnards, no longer raised any objections. The decree of 5 Fructidor (August 22) decided that the electoral assemblies would have to select the two-thirds of the future deputies from among those members of the Convention on the active list. As it was quite likely that some of the assemblies would not obey or that their choice would fall upon the same men, a decree of the thirteenth instructed them to draw up a triple list of deputies, and sitpulated that if they failed to elect 500 members (in point of fact 483, for the deputies for Corsica and the colonies were provisionally maintained in their seats), the required number would be made up by co-optation. In the end, therefore, there had been a partial return to this last method and the Fructidor decrees represented a compromise. But the advantage which the Republicans had counted on obtaining from the retention of the two-thirds was considerably reduced in advance.

The Royalists did not fulminate any the less for that, especially the Feuillants, who included a great many former members of the Constituent and Legislative Assemblies who wanted to return to power, and a great many journalists eager to come to power. The conflict which had been threatening for such a long time finally broke out between them and the Republican Thermidorians, now that, with the terrorists out of the way, they were free to fight for supreme authority. The Monarchists attacked Tallien the Septembrist, "Chénier-Cain," and all the members of the Convention, whom they nicknamed the Immortals; while Lezay-Marnésia, asking why the Commission of Eleven had fixed the number of Directors at five, and the number of Ministers at six, had already replied: "because five and six make Eleven." The Republicans replied by calling their adversaries deserters, Chouans, and agents of Pitt. Madame de Staël was appalled. As Sweden was about to conclude with the Republic a treaty of friendship which was signed on September 29, the Swedish Ambassador, the Baron de Staël, had come back to Paris. "Everybody is talking about Madame de Staël's dinner parties," the *Courrier républicain* reported on 17 Fructidor (September 3). Her salon had become the headquarters of statesmen waiting to be called to power; she had set to work to secure the return of Talleyrand and of Montesquiou, whom, so it was said, she wanted to see appointed Directors. Her policy was to unite the Constitutional Monarchists and the Republicans in order to consolidate the Republic of the Notables. The decree of the two-thirds dashed her hopes to the ground.

The next move was up to the primary assemblies, which

were to be held from 20 Fructidor (September 6) to 10 Vendémiaire (October 2). The Royalists turned their attention to these assemblies in the hope of obtaining control over them with the secret help of the clergy. There is nothing to show, however, that at this time the Royalists were grouped together in a party under a central direction, as would be the case in Year V; admittedly on 29 Fructidor (September 15), the Lepeletier Section decided to send an address to all the communes in France, but if there was any consultation between one region of the country and another it must have been a result of personal relations. It was only in Paris and the surrounding area that Royalist propaganda seems to have been put over in a methodical way. At Beauvais, copies of a printed circular were seized; and while it is impossible to take the word of the Republicans, who blamed every riot on the activity of agents sent out by certain Sections in Paris, one conclusive fact must be noted: when the Royalists of Châteauneuf-en-Thimerais rose in revolt, they lost no time in dispatching commissioners to the Lepeletier Section, which sent them to call on all the other Sections.

For their part, the Convention and its Committees also tried to exert a certain influence on the primary assemblies. They believed that they could count on the support of the army. At Nantes, between 28 and 30 Thermidor (August 15 and 17), the troops had come to blows with the "black collars," and had thrown into the water some Chouans they had just captured; and on 11 Fructidor (August 28), a deputation from the camp outside Paris came and promised loyalty to the Convention. As early as the second (August 19), a circular from the Committee of Public Safety had asked the representatives of the armies to speed up the voting, and as fast as the results came in, it published them in the hope of swaying public opinion. Then again, it did not hesitate to resort once more to measures of exclusion. On 1 Fructidor (August 18), a decree deprived those émigrés who had not obtained complete reinstatement, of their civic rights, a measure which barred them from the primary assemblies. On the fifth *jour complémentaire* (September 21), the relatives of émigrés were ordered to abandon all public employment. An article of the Constitution forbade any new exception to the laws against the émigrés and declared their property to be irrevocably transferred to the nation. Hostility to the non-juring and refractory clergy became very fierce again. On 20 Fructidor (September 6), a fortnight's grace was granted to deportees to go into exile once more, but the laws against them were confirmed and those who failed to comply with them were ordered to be arrested. The Constitution deprived of civic rights those who had joined "any foreign corporation" that implied "distinctions of birth" or required "religious vows." The law on the control of religious worship, passed on 7 Vendémiaire, Year IV (September 29, 1795), introduced into the formula of submission imposed on all priests recognition of the sovereignty of the people, and laid down sentences of two years' imprisonment for any priest who attacked the sale of national property, and imprisonment for life in the hulks for any priest who preached the restoration of the Monarchy. On the other hand, on 15 Fructidor (September 1), the right to vote was conceded to the terrorists, and the following day the Convention annulled the judgments and proceedings of the courts that were directed against members of revolutionary bodies and authorities on account of controls and requisitions ordered by representatives on mission. But the primary assemblies did as they pleased: they admitted the émigrés and excluded the terrorists. When the latter complained, the Convention ignored their protests; on 6 Fructidor (August 23), moreover, it had closed the popular clubs.

The Parisian Sections did not stop at that. They maintained that the government was reinforcing the troops at its disposal in Paris and the surrounding region, and pretended to fear an armed action in the event of the plebiscite giving a negative result. On 20 Fructidor (September 6), the Lepeletier Section passed an act of guarantee placing the citizens under the protection of the Sections, and when all the other Sections had given their support, it proposed, the following day, the formation of a central committee. Although the Convention had banned it, the Fontaine de Grenelle Section nonetheless maintained its approval, and declared itself in permanent session; twelve others followed its example. "I have material proof," declared a member of the Convention on 5 Vendémiaire (September 27), "of the formation of the central committee in Paris." Finally, a great many deputations went and harangued the troops, and not without success: in the Parisian region, the army returned a considerable proportion of negative votes on the decree of the two-thirds.

At the end of Fructidor, the plebiscite was sufficiently advanced for the result to be regarded as established. Although voters were required to answer with a yes or no, over 250 primary assemblies had made observations, very rarely in favor of the Constitution of 1793, and rather more often in favor of the Monarchy; eighty had asked that Catholicism be given back its freedom, or even given a dominant position. The Constitution had been accepted by all the departments, with the exception of the Mont Terrible, which had protested in this way against annexation. But it was not easy to draw any conclusions from this vote for, in Vaucluse for example, only the Royalists had been able to vote and they had given their approval only in order to get rid of the Convention. The decree of the two-thirds had been given a much less favorable reception, and for the same reason. The west, the Parisian region, and all the Sections apart from the Quinze-Vingts in Paris itself had rejected it; Provence had shown strong opposition to it; the Rhône and the Isère had voted against it; the center of France had been divided, while on the other hand the north and the east had produced a strong majority in favor, although the Bas-Rhin and the Doubs had declared themselves against. Altogether, nineteen departments had rejected the decree. Many assemblies had neglected to make any comment on it, so that the mass of abstentions seemed enormous. But here again any interpretation remained problematical. The Convention had not stated explicitly that the plebiscite applied to the decree of the two-thirds, and in any case had not asked for a separate vote. That is why, although the considerable number of abstentions with regard to the Constitution is an important fact, it does not, insofar as the decree is concerned, have the importance which has often been attributed to it: in the uncertainty which the Convention had allowed to remain, perhaps deliberately, about the system of voting, it is possible to argue that those who had accepted the Constitution did not consider it necessary to mention the decree. When it came to the counting of votes, another difficulty arose: at least 269 assemblies had not given the numerical results of the ballot, with the result that their opinion was not taken into account; and this happened to be the case with thirty-three Parisian Sections. Moreover, in the *Moniteur* of 7 Vendémiaire (September 29), Trouvé declared that the omission had covered fraudulent misrepresentation: one Section, he said, had accepted the Constitution almost unanimously, with over a thousand citizens present; on the decree, only 342 had voted, of whom 314 had voted against; however, the official record, omitting these two figures, declared the decree to be unanimously rejected, implying that the same number had voted on it as had voted on the Constitution.

Whatever the truth of the matter, when the Convention had declared, on 1 Vendémiaire, Year IV (September 23, 1795), that the Constitution was accepted by 914,853 votes to 41,892 and the decree of the two-thirds by 167,758 votes to 95,373 (the corrected figures given on the sixth were 1,057,390 to 49,978 and 205,498 to 108,754), eighteen Parisian Sections disputed the result and demanded a re-count, especially in the case of the capital, by the commissioners of the primary assemblies. The agitation spread to the streets, and on the evening of the second, shots were fired at the guard at the Palais Égalité; crowds gathered in several districts. In the night of 3-4 Vendémiaire, the Convention sat until three o'clock, expecting an insurrection. The Bonne Nouvelle Section announced that it had put the terrorists in prison and the Théâtre Français Section that it was going to purge itself of those "monsters." The Convention forbade the jailers to receive them, and forbade the Sections to send out their armed forces; it was not obeyed.

On the ninth (October 1), the news of the rising in the Thymerais brought the revolt to a head. On 27 Fructidor

(September 13), the primary assembly of Châteauneuf had risen in revolt and had seized the public treasury. A crowd formed, raising the *fleurs de lys* flag. Dreux, called to the rescue, sent a contingent. The representatives on mission at Chartres reoccupied that town, from which a detachment led by Bourdon marched on Nonancourt: the rebels were routed, leaving ten of their number dead. The Lepeletier Section immediately called upon all the electors in Paris to assemble on 11 Vendémiaire (October 3) at the Théâtre Français to protest against this massacre, asking: "Are we going to see a recurrence of those days of horror and carnage we have lived through?" But only about a hundred electors, belonging to some fifteen Sections, turned up. The former magistrate Lebois, president of the Théâtre Français, and Lacretelle and Fiévée harangued them until nightfall: when the military arrived during the evening, the hall was empty. All the same, according to the report which Merlin de Douai read out on 14 Vendémiaire, seven Sections which he named and some others as well had raised the flag of revolt during this time. The Convention declared itself in permanent session and set up an extraordinary Commission of Five to organize their defense; Barras was the strong man on this body.

They had not many troops at their disposal: barely 4,000 men in the suburbs who, for the most part, were sent off every day in detachments; 3,000 more, sent for from Saint-Omer, arrived too late. After the *journées* of Prairial, the Sections had handed over their cannons, but they were at the camp at Les Sablons. To obtain reinforcements, the Commission appealed to the officers removed by Aubry, and above all decided to enroll the *sans-culottes*: 1,500 "patriots of '89" formed three battalions. On 12 Vendémiaire (October 4) the Convention revoked the decree of 21 Germinal on the disarming of the terrorists, and that of 5 Ventôse which had placed under surveillance the government officials dismissed after Thermidor. Although the Law of Suspects had been revoked at the same time, this caused an indescribable sensation and rallied a host of waverers to the rebels: the terrorists had to be dealt with and consequently the Convention too, since it was taking them into its service.

As usual, the Lepeletier Section took the initiative; it had the news given out to the rolling of a drum and called on the citizens of Paris to take arms. The *rappel* was beaten; the shops were closed; a good many Republicans were arrested and assumed that they were doomed to be killed; in point of fact, on the thirteenth, about a hundred musket shots were fired at the Prison de la Force where the prisoners armed themselves with logs to defend their lives. The Five ordered Menou, the head of the military force, to occupy the hall of the Lepeletier Section, in the convent of the Filles Saint-Thomas, where the Stock Exchange now stands. Now it happened that Menou sympathized with the rebels: he had just protested against the decrees of the twelfth and had refused to place the patriots under his command; his troops did not set off until half-past nine in the evening; when they reached the Section, with the representative Laporte, the president, Delalot, offered to send his members away if they withdrew, and Menou agreed. The Convention stripped him of his command, but it was too late to send fresh troops: the Sections were on the move and coming to the help of their colleagues. The leaders set up a central commission under Richer-Serizy; the Committees were outlawed, an extraordinary court established, and the

Treasury occupied. The military command was given to Danican, a former Hébertist who had gone over to the reaction, and who had written a letter, published by the *Moniteur* on 5 Fructidor, which called for a purge of the army; sent in disgrace from Rouen to Dieppe, he had resigned and had just arrived in Paris.

The greater part of the capital had escaped from the Convention, which indeed found itself in a state of siege. On 13 Vendémiaire (October 5), at half-past four in the morning, Barras was given the task of organizing resistance, and Generals Bonaparte, Carteaux, Brune, Loison and Dupont were placed at his disposal. Bonaparte was not appointed second in command, as he later related; but he acted as if he had been. Murat was sent to Les Sablons and brought back the cannons that were there. The Louvre and the Tuileries were fortified and the guns positioned so as to cover all the streets leading to the Carrousel; Carteaux occupied the embankment and the approach to the Pont-Neuf. At the end of the morning, Danican, coming from the Left Bank, pushed him back and joined up with the Right Bank where the Sections, under the command of the émigré Lafond, were marching on the Tuileries. There were about twenty thousand of them; having no cannons, they tried to win over the defenders of the Convention by inviting them to fraternize. As Barras had forbidden his forces to open fire first, the danger was undeniable. In the assembly, the Right was trying to intervene. In the evening of the twelfth and about three o'clock on the thirteenth, it suggested at the very least modifying the decree on the re-arming of the terrorists. But all of a sudden musket firing started without anybody knowing exactly where. After some fierce fighting, the Sections were repulsed all along the line;

Danican tried to take the Republicans in the rear by advancing along the Left Bank; caught in a cross fire of grapeshot from a position at the end of the rue de Beaune and from Carteaux's troops on the Right Bank, he had to withdraw. At nightfall, Barras took the offensive and occupied the Palais Égalité. In the rue Honoré, however, the Sections remained in possession of the Church of Saint-Roch until the following day, and it is just a legend that depicts them shot down by gunfire from Bonaparte stationed on the steps of the church. On the fourteenth, columns of troops crossed the city without meeting any resistance; the rebels had retired to their homes and the leaders were in hiding or on the run. There had been between two and three hundred killed on each side.

The repression was very moderate. As early as the fourteenth, there were complaints in the Convention that the Committees were releasing crowds of prisoners. On the fifteenth, three military commissions were set up, but sentence of death was pronounced only on the leaders and the "agitators in writing," in other words the journalists. In point of fact, most of the accused were sentenced in their absence and no attempt was made to find them. Only Lebois and Lafond were executed. As for Menou, he was acquitted. The *journée* of the thirteenth of Vendémiaire nonetheless had the effect of giving the government complete control of the capital. Henceforth the city was placed under military occupation. The National Guard was disarmed, and its cavalry, artillery, crack companies, and general staff abolished; it was subordinated to the commander of the garrison and to the general of the home army, who was Bonaparte. The revolutionary role of Paris was at an end.

At least the danger they had run had revived revolutionary feelings once again in the Thermidorians of the Center and had put them back in the frame of mind they had shown after the fall of Robespierre, when they had called for the reconciliation of all Republicans; thus they finished as they had begun, which is another reason why the *journée* of the thirteenth of Vendémiaire is important. On the twentieth, it was decided to reinstate the officers removed by Aubry, and on 3 Brumaire (October 25), on the other hand, to purge the army of the counterrevolutionary elements that he had introduced into it. As early as 15 Vendémiaire, the patriots of '89 had been disbanded, but now the Convention began to pass, not without a certain hesitation, measures of reparation in favor of the Jacobins: on the twentieth, the indictment of Barère was revoked; on the twenty-second (October 14), sentences and current proceedings against the patriots, for actions which were not punishable under the penal code, were annulled, and orders were given for their release; on the twenty-first, all prosecutions based on arrests carried out under the Law of Suspects were forbidden and sentences pronounced on this account were annulled. It was the fate of the imprisoned deputies which remained longest in doubt; the Convention pardoned them only on 4 Brumaire (October 26), just as it was dissolving its last meeting, by passing a general amnesty for "acts simply connected with the Revolution," the offenses against common law being set apart and the émigrés being excluded together with the deportees, the accused of Vendémiaire and the manufacturers of counterfeit *assignats*. The decree of 5 Fructidor, which declared the arrested Montagnards ineligible, nonetheless remained in force, as forming part of the Constitution.

In the meantime, an offensive had been launched against the reactionaries. On 19 Vendémiaire (October 11), Fréron was sent to the south of France to stamp out the White Terror, and on the twenty-ninth, Chénier referred to the Committees an inquiry into the conduct of Chambon and Cadroy. On the twenty-third, after Delaunay had read out his report on the papers seized at the lawyer Lemaître's house, which proved complicity between the Vendémiaire rebels and the émigrés, Tallien reproached him for not having named the compromised deputies, and got the assembly to go into secret session. He then accused Rovère and Saladin, whose arrest was decreed the next day. On the thirtieth (October 22), Letourneur's report on the operations of the Rhine armies was the occasion for a fresh batch of charges: a decree was issued for the arrest of Aubry and three others, including Miranda, the Venezuelan adventurer formerly known as Lieutenant de Dumouriez, who had been imprisoned during the Terror and rightly suspected, for he had never ceased to be in communication with the English. None of these people in fact came to any harm, and a few days later they all benefited by the amnesty.

Soon after the electoral assemblies had met on 20 Vendémiaire (October 12), it became obvious that the Convention was getting excited to no avail and that in the next Legislature the Right would be more powerful than ever. Only 379 members of the Convention were re-elected, of whom 124 were substitutes, and nearly all of them were moderates or suspected Royalists, including Defermon, Boissy d'Anglas and Lanjuinais, Larivière and Durand-Maillane, Rovère and Saladin, whose arrest had recently been decreed. As for the new Third, the majority was made up of Royalists and Catholics; in Paris, for example, the electors had returned Dambray, the future Chancellor of Louis XVIII; Portalis, who would be Director of Religious Worship after the Concordat; and the banker Lecoulteux de Canteleu, a Feuillant. The turncoat Montagnards who, after making themselves the leaders of the reaction, had been blocking its way since Fructidor—Tallien, Fréron, Legendre, Bourdon and Dubois-Crancé—were beaten and could be sure that the re-elected moderates would leave them to their fate, as did indeed happen with most of them. Now the election was of dubious legality, since the émigrés had been allowed to vote while the Jacobins had been excluded. Consequently several members of the Convention proposed that the results be set aside. On 30 Vendémiaire (October 22), after Daunou, ignoring this proposal, had got the rules of procedure for the installation of the Legislature passed, Bentabole suggested that at least the re-elected members of the Convention should immediately divide into two chambers to elect the Directory, without waiting for the new Third. He was referred to the provisions of the Constitution. Tallien, coming out into the open, promptly declared that "if they did not get rid of the Royalists in the government and the courts, the counter-revolution would be carried out constitutionally within three months' time," and suggested asking the Commission of Five to decide what measures should be taken "to save the country." Merlin de Douai, on their behalf, declined the task, and a special committee of five was appointed, including Tallien. But the former Girondins, Republicans though they were, refused to follow him and return to a revolutionary government by violating the Constitution. On 1 Brumaire (October 23), Thibaudeau denounced the plots which were being hatched for the arrest of the deputies of the Right who had previously been denounced, the annulment of the elections and the postponement of the meeting of the Legislature. He attacked Tallien the Septembrist, the person chiefly responsible for the Royalist reaction, whom an intercepted letter from Louis XVIII laid open to suspicion himself. Tallien gave way under the attack, and, not daring to admit his plans, confined himself to proposing that the Convention should declare itself in permanent session, a proposal to which Thibaudeau replied by demanding that the Commission of Five should report immediately before breaking up. He won the day without any difficulty: on the third, Tallien contented himself with getting the émigrés and also their relatives excluded from public employment under pain of exile. The way therefore remained open for the new constitutional experiment. Although the moderate Republicans had remained within the law, they were not blind to the dangers threatening them, so that they persisted, to a certain extent, in no longer seeing any enemies on the Left—on condition, of course, that the democrats confined themselves to supporting them and made no attempt to compete with them for power. It was under these auspices that the Directory was installed: the election of Carnot was proof of that.

The volte-face of the Republican Thermidorians, consecrated by the *journée* of 13 Vendémiaire, had another far-reaching consequence: it allowed the annexationists to resume the war on the Rhine and to obtain union with Belgium. Aubry had left the Committee on 15 Thermidor (August 2); true, Threilhard followed him, but Sieyès and Reubell came back on the Committee as did Letourneur and Merlin de Douai, whom they won over. Thus the majority of the diplomatic section found itself determined to extend the frontier to the Rhine; the *Moniteur* published Roberjot's report on his mission in the occupied regions, which concluded in favor of union with France, and petitions to this effect were obtained from the Rhenish population. The negotiations with the Germans promptly came to an end. On July 29, the Emperor, in ratifying the Diet's *conclusum* in favor of negotiations, had specified that the integrity of the empire had to be respected; at Basle, Hardenberg repeatedly declared that Prussia would not go beyond the treaty of April 5 if France did not give up her claim to the Rhine; when, on August 3, Frederick William was notified of the third partition of Poland, he was therefore obliged, not wishing to make common cause with the Republicans, to resign himself to accepting it in principle, while at the same time insisting on a larger share. After some stormy conferences, he contented himself with what he was offered, namely the region situated to the south of East Prussia, including Warsaw. The Committee of Public Safety continued to throw out feelers toward Austria, but Thugut refused to take part in discussions without England's support. On September 28, Russia joined the Coalition. Against England, France secured in theory an alliance with Sweden, but to turn theory into fact, she would have had to be able to send Sweden money. Godoy showed readiness to accept an agreement of this sort; but as a commercial treaty was asked for in addition, the whole project came to nothing.

Determined to keep its conquests, the Committee decided to give categorical orders to the generals, and on 20 Fructidor (September 6), the Army of the Sambre and Meuse, under Jourdan's command, crossed the Rhine at Düsseldorf and Neuwied; Clerfayt retreated step by step as far as the Main. At the end of July, Wurmser had brought up a new army to the upper Rhine; from there, in September he simply sent Quasdanovitch northward with 12,000 men, to maintain liaison and cover the huge stores at Heidelberg. Pichegru's role could have been decisive: if he had emerged from Mannheim, Clerfayt would have been surrounded, but he was not ready and his troops remained strung out from Basle to Mainz. Not until 13 Fructidor (September 16) did he concentrate two weak divisions, 12,000 men in all, leaving Mannheim the next day to advance on Heidelberg. Quasdanovitch was there already and launched a vigorous attack on September 23; one of the French divisions merely bombarded his troops, while the other was put to flight. However, this diversion had been sufficient to draw Clerfayt away towards the Neckar, so that Jourdan was able to take the Main line and complete the blockade of Mainz, while Marceau was laying siege to Ehrenbreitstein. By working together, Jourdan and Pichegru could still manage to defeat Clerfayt; a specific order had been necessary to decide Wurmser to go to his help and he was still a long way away. On September 27, the two French generals had a meeting and decided to wait for the Committee's orders, which failed to arrive.

It must be assumed that it was too busy keeping an eye on the Parisian Sections; all the same, it found time to prepare the annexation of Belgium. On 8 Vendémiaire (September 30), Merlin de Douai put the proposal for annexation to the Convention, setting forth at the same time the plebiscites of 1793, the economic advantages of annexation, and the need to make sure of a good strategic frontier. Harmand de la Meuse and Lesage objected that Austria would never resign herself to this loss; besides, the

Belgians were too different from the French, in their way of life and their religious ideas, ever to be assimilated; their supposed desire for union with France was worthless, since it had not been freely expressed. Lesage was particularly aggressive, maintaining that the Belgians were happy under their old Constitution, and that they should be returned to Austria or given their independence. "It was typical of the Mountain to obtain votes with the sword and issue decrees without thinking. . . . How can the Committee be so blind about such projects? . . . How can it make itself the agent of brigands?" This Girondin was forgetting that it was his party which, at the end of 1792, had made annexations the order of the day, and in linking this question with home affairs, he was stating in advance that the thirteenth of Vendémiaire would also determine foreign policy. On the ninth, Merlin de Douai and Roberjot returned to the attack and Carnot gave them his support. They carried the proposal. Merlin had also spoken in favor of the Rhine frontier, but he had postponed any decision until a general peace had been declared.

Soon afterward, military events revealed that peace was anything but imminent. At the beginning of October, Wurmser appeared before Mannheim with 55,000 men, and on the tenth, Clerfayt managed to cross the Main. He turned Jourdan's flank by violating the demarcation line, and pushed him back towards the Lann. Pichegru did not budge. On October 29, he finally received the order to attack. It was too late. The same day, Clerfayt routed the division blockading Mainz and liberated the town. Jourdan had already fallen back on Düsseldorf and was crossing the Rhine. Going up the valley at the beginning of November, the Austrians forced Pichegru to retreat behind the Queich, and on the twenty-first they recaptured Mannheim.

In speaking out definitely in favor of the annexations, the Republican Thermidorians had finally broken with the Royalists, but they had been unable either to make peace or to wage war, and on the frontier as at home they bequeathed nothing but dangers and difficulties to the Directory.

CHAPTER ELEVEN

The Achievement
of the Thermidorians

The Convention broke up on 4 Brumaire, Year IV (October 26, 1795), after sitting for over three years and studding its existence with some of the most striking contradictions in the history of parliamentary assemblies. The Thermidorians were guilty of some of these contradictions and their reputation stands very low because there was a certain duplicity in their conduct: they inveighed against the despotic actions of the revolutionary government, but, when dealing with their adversaries, they paid little attention to the law; they denounced the Red Terror, but they organized or tolerated a White Terror; they vilified the intervention of the State in the economy, but they gave a free reign to businessmen greedy for scandalous speculation, and to corrupt deputies. Even historians hostile to the Montagnards admit that there was neither beauty nor grandeur in the reign of their enemies.

However, in favor of the Thermidorians, it can be pleaded that the great majority of them were honest men and that they suffered from a lack of first-class leaders. The spirit of vengeance raging around them could not, humanly speaking, completely fail to affect them, and yet more than once they tried to resist it. They were faced with insurmountable difficulties, at a time when the guillotine and exile had deprived them of leaders. Drifting along usually on the current of events, they nonetheless had definite ideas about the form of government which ought to be set up in France; if they were unable to organize it in its entirety, the Directory and the Consulate would, in many respects, simply continue their work. That is why, removed from the ephemeral tumult of political conflict and replaced in a historical perspective, the period is seen to have been both meaningful and important: going back beyond the attempt at social democracy that the Montagnards were led into by the requirements of the struggle against the Revolutions' enemies, the Thermidorians linked up again with the tradition bequeathed by the Constituent Assembly, which condemned both the *ancien régime* and democracy, to insure the predominance of the bourgeoisie whose rise to power, prepared for by the entire history of France and sanctioned by its capabilities, could alone, in its opinion, insure the prosperity of the national community.

Constitutional Monarchists and Republicans were no

doubt divided as to the title and powers to be conferred on
the chief of the Executive; above all, the former wanted
him to be hereditary and the latter, elected; this disagree-
ment weighed heavily on the history of the period and that
of the nineteenth century. But the Thermidorians, when
preparing the Constitution of Year III, were agreed that
it was incumbent upon the "notables" to rule and govern,
and the cardinal principle of their activity had to be to
maintain liberty and equality before the law, so that the
ranks of the bourgeoisie should remain open to all who
were destined to rise in society as a result of their merit,
work, or good fortune. It might also be added that the
Constituent Assembly, chiefly preoccupied as it was with
overthrowing the *ancien régime*, had shown more verbal
generosity towards the lower classes, more confidence in
their virtues, and more hope too in a social evolution, which
liberty would be sufficient to render fruitful and peaceful.
In Year II, the bourgeoisie had seen itself deprived of
power: the nationalization of the economy had dried up
the main sources of its wealth, and the Montagnards, who
had sprung from its own ranks, had put themselves at the
head of the *sans-culottes*. It had been frightened, and could
not forget it. That is why, with its attention concentrated
henceforth on its own defense, it became hard and gloomy
in spirit. Its distrust of and contempt for the common
people were revived, and were intensified by a rancor sometimes bordering on hate; very little was needed to trans-
form the bourgeoisie into a new aristocracy which would
work unscrupulously to keep for itself all the benefits of the
Revolution. It was during the Thermidorian period, in a
reaction against the spirit of Year II, that there awoke in

the upper ranks of the French bourgeoisie that class consciousness which became more and more exclusive, and which ended up by typifying the July Monarchy.

Let us listen to Boissy d'Anglas justifying the property qualification for suffrage:

> We must be governed by the best citizens; the best citizens are those who are most educated and most interested in the keeping of the law. Now, with very few exceptions, you will find such men only among those who possess some property, who are attached to the country that contains it, the laws that protect it, and the peace that maintains it; men who owe to that property and to the affluence it affords the education which has made them fit to discuss, wisely and equitably, the advantages and the drawbacks of the laws that determine the fate of the country. . . . A country governed by landowners is in the social order, whereas one governed by persons other than property owners is in a state of nature.

As for Dupont de Nemours, he rose to metaphysical heights:

> It is obvious that the property owners, without whose consent nobody in the country would have either food or lodging, are that country's leading citizens. They are sovereigns by the grace of God, of Nature, of their work, of their progress, and of the work and progress of their ancestors.

Admittedly, none of this was new, and Dupont, in particular, spoke as the Physiocrats had spoken in the past. In substance, some members of the Third Estate had said the same thing in the Constituent Assembly, but never in this dogmatic tone and never without meeting any contradiction. Madame de Staël, demanding the monopoly of power for the notables, claimed to be uniting in their ranks men of merit and men of wealth; Bonaparte would pride himself on reserving a place for talent. With Dupont de Nemours, the mask dropped, and Boissy was really no less explicit in his intervention in the debate on the foundation of central schools: he obtained a reduction in the number of these schools, explaining that to raise the number would be to incur the danger of increasing "the parasitical and ambitious minority." As far as possible, what we call secondary education was to be reserved for the children of property owners.

The Thermidorians did not have time to give the bourgeoisie, at the same time as a political constitution, the social charter which it would receive in the form of the Civil Code. The bill, tabled on 23 Fructidor, Year II (September 9, 1794)—the second project of its kind—remained in abeyance. But they dealt an initial blow at the laws of succession of Year II, which aimed at systematically splitting up inheritances, by abolishing the retroactive effect on 9 Fructidor, Year III (August 26, 1795). They also passed a mortgage code on 9 Messidor (June 27). The re-establishment of imprisonment for debt was already being called for, by such bodies as the Bonne Nouvelle Section on 24 Thermidor (August 11). The change in morals and above all the emancipation of women also aroused anxiety. Corruption had not increased to anything like the extent that certain historians, and consequently most novelists, suggest, simply because they consider only "society," in other words a few hundred wealthy families. On the contrary it is clear that morals, and above all the concept of what they ought to be, had not developed at all as one would have imagined under the influence of the liberal principles proclaimed in 1789, especially as far as women were concerned. The French people, on the whole, went on living as they had always lived. The Jacobins had often been puritans, and rarely feminists. The *Catéchisme du citoyen* in which Volney in 1793 had laid down the moral obligations of the good Republican was extremely traditionalist, particularly as far as the family was concerned. This discrepancy would soon awaken the rancor of certain women—notably Madame de Staël—and the emancipation of women, at least on the emotional level, would be one of the features of Romanticism. In spite of everything, some women had nonetheless been seen taking an interest in politics and neglecting their homes for the club, the tribune and even the riot. Divorces were quite frequent; nobles and bourgeois had resorted to them when they emigrated, in order to save their property by transferring it to their former wives who remained in France, and in many cases the pretended separation had become real and final. In Paris, at least, the salons of Madame Tallien and Madame Hamelin were anything but schools of virtue for the upper middle class. The Thermidorians ended up by becoming alarmed at this weakening of marital and paternal authority and the damage caused to the "standing" of the bourgeois family by the dissolute conduct of women; at least, on 15 Thermidor (August 2), they suspended the laws of 8 Nivôse and 4 Floréal, Year II, which had made divorce easier.

However, on one essential point—the influence of religious ideas—the Thermidorian Republicans did not act as the precursors of the Consulate. Admittedly it can be maintained that by restoring to a certain point the free practice of religion, they allowed the religious revival which culminated in the Concordat to make its initial progress.

and alms-houses on 9 Fructidor, Year III (August 26). It was only too easy to justify the indifference shown toward national assistance by the shortage of funds. It was a different matter for education, but in this sphere as well, the necessary economies served as a pretext for reaction.

The Thermidorians displayed a proper solicitude for the great scientific establishments which the Montagnards had begun to set up. On 1 Brumaire, Year III (October 22, 1794), they opened the School of Public Services, intended to train engineers for the army, the navy and public works; on 6 Vendémiaire, Year IV (September 28, 1795), it became the Central School of Public Works; presently, it is the École Polytechnique, or Military Academy of Artillery and Engineering. The Conservatoire des Arts et Métiers, or School of Arts and Crafts, was installed on 19 Vendémiaire, Year III (October 10, 1794), at Saint-Martin-des-Champs, and a school of clockmaking created at Besançon in Messidor. On 14 Frimaire, Year III (December 4, 1794), plans had been approved for three schools of medicine, and the Deaf and Dumb Institute was founded on 16 Nivôse (January 5, 1795). The Museum, founded on June 10, 1793, was reorganized and Cuvier joined it in 1795. The decree of 7 Messidor, Year III (June 25, 1795) gave birth to the Bureau des Longitudes or Central Astronomical Office, and classes in astronomy were initiated at the Observatory. The School of Oriental Languages dates from 10 Germinal (March 30). Archeology and the arts also came in for their share: Grégoire's reports and the activities of the temporary Commission of Arts, of which Alexandre Lenoir was the moving spirit, led to the formation of the Museum of French Monuments at the Augustins and at the Louvre, on 15 Fructidor (September

1); archeological classes on inscriptions and medallions were begun at the Bibliothèque Nationale. The preparation of the metric system continued: on 1 Vendémiaire, Year IV (September 23, 1795), use of the meter was made compulsory in Paris and the department of the Seine, as of the beginning of Nivôse; on 28 Thermidor (August 15), the franc had become the monetary unit. Finally, just before breaking up on 3 Brumaire, Year IV (October 25, 1795), the Convention placed at the head of the country's establishments of higher education, in order to provide them with unified guidance, the Institut National, in which, beside a department of literature and fine arts, it also provided for one for the physical and mathematical sciences and one for the moral and political sciences; the latter was a considerable innovation.

This splendid efflorescence was the consecration of the great intellectual movement of the eighteenth century, and particularly of the efforts of the Encyclopedists and of Condorcet. But only the organization of a system of secondary education could provide the world of learning with a public and interest the sons of the bourgeoisie in the liberal professions which were to offer them a lucrative career. For the Republican State, it was of prime importance that this education should not be left to private initiative or even to local authorities, for this would enable the Roman Church gradually to secure a monopoly for itself once more. In the opinion of the scientists and philosophers, it was not enough to put the former colleges under central control; deprived of their property and their old teachers, they were in a wretched state of stagnation. They were unevenly distributed, and the education given in them, despite a few improvements, was out of keeping with modern thought and the new society. It was almost entirely devoted to the humanities; as for the sciences, only mathematics at the very most was given a place; often, too, the French language was not included in the curriculum. On 6 Ventôse, Year III (February 24, 1795), acting on a report by Lakanal, the Convention therefore created the "central schools" at the rate of one to each department. The curriculum of the three years' course was laid down by the decree and henceforth included French, history, the experimental sciences, law, drawing, and, as far as possible, modern languages. However, this national system of education remained decentralized, partly so that the State should not have to pay for it; the departmental administration bore the cost of it and was allowed to appoint the schoolmasters from among the candidates approved by a board of education. From the technical point of view, the curriculum was too ambitious and the organization unsuited to the needs of children coming from primary school. The three years of the course were independent of one another; the pupils picked the classes they wished to attend; there were no preparatory classes to inculcate the rudiments of each subject, nor any provision for boarding. In theory the central schools were more like the modern universities than the modern *lycées*; between them and the primary school there was a gap, as if the State had wanted only the rich to be able to fill it, by means of private tutors; what is more, education in these central schools was not free.

As for the primary school, the State had at first taken responsibility for it by the law of 27 Brumaire, Year III (November 17, 1794). The teachers were to be housed in the nationalized presbyteries and paid by the Republic;

unfortunately, it was found impossible to provide a school for every commune, and for reasons of economy several villages were grouped in a single school district, a measure which made it difficult to keep the law on compulsory attendance, in spite of the fact that schooling was free. The choice of teachers also remained decentralized; the department appointed them after an examination carried out by a board of education.

The enforcement of this law was far from perfect when, on 3 Brumaire, Year IV (October 25, 1795), the Convention replaced it with another law which revealed the regression of democratic ideas. There was no longer any mention of compulsory attendance and the teacher ceased to be paid by the State: he was left only his lodging, and for the rest he had to return to a salary fixed by the municipality and paid by the parents. It was easy to see that, as had already happened with poor relief, primary education would soon sink back into the same state as at the end of the *ancien régime*. Moreover, the recruiting of teachers was presenting insurmountable difficulties. On 19 Vendémiaire, Year III (October 10, 1794), a training college had been opened which functioned from January to May, 1795. The districts sent 1,300 young men to it to attend lectures given by eminent professors; it was intended that, on their return, they should form the staff of training colleges in the departments, but this project was abandoned. As for the decadal religion which was supposed to act as an extension of school, it had not been organized by the time the Directory came to power.

The central and primary schools were entirely secular, and although priests were not forbidden to teach in them, religious teaching was banned; morality, in the eyes of the ideologists, was based on social utility and on reason. But the Thermidorians did not give them a monopoly of education, so that in many places their secular teaching made parents prefer the independent schools, which in actual fact were Catholic ones. This question of freedom of education was not debated until 28 Brumaire, Year III (November 18, 1794); it was not seriously taken up by the Montagnards, but they expressed some anxiety about the teaching which would be given by the masters in the private schools. In their opinion, the latter should have been placed under the supervision of the authorities; they suggested that it would be advisable to check their qualifications and to compel them to follow a definite curriculum and use certain elementary books. The Thermidorians brushed these objections aside, displaying an indifference which is rather surprising in view of their anticlericalism. Their underlying motives are shown by the reception they gave to Duhem's speech: "I am afraid that the public schools might become, with regard to the private schools, what the poor schools used to be with regard to those which demanded fees; I am afraid that they may be attended only by the children of the *sans-culottes* and that the rich will send their children to the other schools." "May I ask," retorted Dubois-Crancé, "if an attempt is being made to prevent a father from educating his son as he wishes?" and Lecomte declared: "The previous speaker is so attached to the egalitarian system which he wants to establish at all costs, that he cannot bear one citizen having more merit than another." These debating courtesies allowed the Thermidorians to refrain from admitting that they wanted to reserve for the bourgeoisie the opportunity to keep their children away from the national school where they would have found themselves sitting beside the children of the poor; class consciousness had won the day over anticlericalism.

While the Thermidorians were thus beginning, by legal methods, a social reaction which was not to come to a stop for a long time, they simultaneously set off, by giving way to inflation, a social upheaval which would bring about a profound change in the structure of the bourgeoisie. During the summer of 1795 it was already visible. The collapse of the *assignat* ruined the rentiers and the government officials. Just as taxpayers and purchasers of national property lost no time in liquidating their debts to the State by means of valueless paper money, so debtors paid off, at almost no cost to themselves, not only the interest but the capital sum of their mortgages. On 25 Messidor (July 13, 1795), the Convention suspended the possibility of repaying the capital sum of mortgages taken out before January 1, 1792, and banned anticipated repayment for all others; but this was only an imperfect remedy. Conversely, it had to forbid sellers, on 14 Fructidor (August 31), to claim back their former property, many courts having acceded to applications for the annulment of contracts and dispossessed the purchasers. Landed property, which at that time formed the principal wealth of the bourgeois who "lived nobly" and even of the others, also suffered considerably. It was real estate that was ill-treated most of all. The decree of 3 Messidor (June 21) stipulated that rents should be paid in *assignats* at par, whereas farm rents should be paid at the rate of six to one; the decree of 2 Thermidor (July 20) was even more advantageous to country landlords in that it granted half of farm rents in kind. It was then that the housing crisis worsened in Paris and the big cities, where the population was rapidly swollen by the return of city dwellers who, in 1793 and 1794, had emigrated or taken refuge in the country, as also by the influx of people who wanted to take advantage of government distributions and the sale of cheap bread; building and repairs came to a stop and the congestion became irremediable during the following winter. However, it would be a mistake to have any illusions about the fate of landed property. The farmers were only obliged to pay half their farm rents and taxes in kind if they had a surplus, and they did not fail to get rid of such surpluses surreptitiously or to plead market requisitions in order to be able to pay in *assignats* only. It is true that in the greater part of France it was the *métayage* system, by which the farmer paid rent in kind, which predominated, and it necessarily made considerable progress, since the landlord, on the expiration of a farming lease, naturally preferred, in the prevailing conditions, a concession with a share in the produce. However, as early as Year II he had been hit by another device. The tenant farmer leased the livestock and farm equipment from him, on condition that the farmer return it when he gave up the lease or reimbursed its value. He did not fail to sell everything and liquidate his debt, at the price of the incoming inventory, in depreciated *assignats*. On 2 Thermidor, Year II (July 20, 1794), the Montagnard Committee of Public Safety had obliged him to pay for the livestock in kind, and on 17 Fructidor (August 31), the Thermidorian Committee extended this rule to the equipment of the estate. These decrees were confirmed by the decree of 15 Germinal, Year III (April 3, 1795), but it is doubtful whether the landlords were able to make use of them in most cases. On 10 Floréal (April 29), a deputy consequently demanded the annulment of all leases, but without success.

Without the slightest doubt, the revolutionary bourgeois were sorely tried by the consequences of inflation, and that must have contributed not a little to thinning their ranks. However, among the commoners who had put their fortune into government stocks or land, in order to live a life of leisure, supporters of the Monarchy and even of the *ancien régime* were probably in a majority. Their ruin was added to that of so many others who, like the privileged classes, had been stripped of their feudal rights or had seen their property confiscated as a result of emigration or convictions. The social revolution, brought about by the revolutionary laws, was therefore completed after Year III by the revolution produced by inflation, and in most cases it weakened the influence of those Frenchmen who were hostile to the Republic and even to the work of the Constituent Assembly.

The bourgeoisie, taken as a whole, could have been deprived by the monetary disaster of a considerable part of its capital and thus hampered in its economic progress. In point of fact, nothing of the sort happened. First of all it must be pointed out that the disaster could not reach the same proportions as in our time, because the personal estate as yet occupied only a modest place; if the landed proprietors were impoverished, they were generally able to retain their property and wait for better days; moreover, many of them made good their losses by buying national property cheap. Even if this had not been the case, their class would not have been diminished as a result. The members of the old bourgeoisie who disappeared gave place to others; even before the Terror, and above all after 1795, war supplies and speculation of all sorts—in *assignats* and currency, in merchandise and national property—pushed into the forefront a host of adventurers of whom a certain number succeeded in consolidating their gains and founding bourgeois families. These *nouveaux riches* were far inferior to those of the eighteenth century as far as moral and intellectual culture was concerned. They had no respect for disinterested research and no understanding of revolutionary idealism; a narrow, limited utilitarianism was their law, and for a long time they retained, from their origins, a fierce, unscrupulous and almost innocent eagerness to take advantage of all the chances offered to them by troubled times and the unlimited liberty which the Thermidorians had restored to the economy. But if boldness and a capacity for enterprise do not necessarily form part of such characters, it must be admitted that they are very often stimulated by these qualities. It was men such as these who, in the eleventh century, with the help of the revival of trade, had been the first bourgeois, and every monetary and economic crisis, every period in which production alters in order to increase, sees the appearance of fresh examples. Without them the bourgeoisie would waste away, for after a few generations the descendants of the *parvenu* stop working and try to join the aristocracy. The *nouveaux riches* of Year III provided the bourgeoisie with a strength and, as it were, a new blood which prevented it from ossifying. It was from their ranks that, under the Directory and Napoleon's rule, there came many of the leading businessmen who, pressing on with the industrial renovation begun on the English model at the end of the *ancien régime*, were the initiators of modern capitalism in France. In this respect, the Thermidorian period was no doubt simply the dawn of a new age; it is nonetheless important to recognize that dawn.

Nor was it unimportant for the future of the bourgeoisie that the decomposition of the rural community should speed up under the influence of the revolutionary laws, and inflation contributed to this process as well. Year III was a period of triumph for the big farmers; relieved of the *maximum* and of requisitioning, they sold their produce at high prices, and the country took its revenge on the town; at the same time, they paid taxes, farm rents, and the price of national property in worthless *assignats*. They rapidly rose above the common herd of small-holders, *métayers* and day-laborers, to form a peasant bourgeoisie which, producing in order to sell, joined the capitalist ranks.

Consciously or not, the Thermidorians therefore strengthened the social predominance of the bourgeoisie at the same time that they gave it political authority. But on this last point, by requiring it to govern according to liberal rules and with frequent elections, they compromised its future. They doubtless had the best intentions, and in this respect men like Daunou and Chénier showed themselves to be true sons of the eighteenth century. Unfortunately they were also ahead of their time. The Revolution was essentially of a social order and the dispossessed were to go on fighting for a long time yet, with the support of the foreign aristocracy, before resigning themselves. Charette and Stofflet remained in arms. In the south of France, Job Aimé who, as president of the primary assembly of Valence, had forbidden the electors to recognize the decrees of Fructidor, organized an insurrection with the help of the Marquis de Lestang; they seized Montélimar and Avignon and held out there for a few days. In the spring, the war was going to begin again. To their successors who had to wage it, the Thermidorians left no resources other than an almost worthless *assignat* and broken-down armies. To have any chance of governing constitutionally without putting the Revolution in peril, the rulers of France would have had to conclude a general peace, and, declaring themselves annexationists, the Republicans of Year III had been unable to do this. In the coming elections, the Directory would therefore be confronted with the same problem that had faced the Montagnards and the Thermidorians themselves. The former had boldly solved it by means of the dictatorship of a democratic Convention. It was truly ironical that, having repudiated that dictatorship, the Thermidorians, as soon as their Constitution had been passed, found themselves reduced to adulterating its application by the introduction into the Legislature of a majority of members of the Convention. But embarrassed by this very contradiction, and lacking the necessary boldness, they had not dared to choose those members. The result was a disguised dictatorship, which was ineffective and which yet sufficed to ruin the prestige of the new Constitution. In any case, even if the Thermidorians had entrusted the reins of power to reliable members of the Convention, they would have found themselves faced with the same difficulty at the elections of Year V. What followed is common knowledge: they got out of the difficulty on the eighteenth of Fructidor, by means of a *coup d'état* which, this time openly violating their own Constitution, re-established the revolutionary dictatorship. As it was impossible for them to appeal to the people, they carried out this *coup d'état* with the help of the army, and thus their policy ended up by turning the revolutionary dictatorship into a military one.

BIBLIOGRAPHICAL SUGGESTIONS

On the sources, see: P. CARON, *Manuel pratique pour l'étude de la Révolution* (Paris, 1912, 2nd ed., 1947); C. SCHMIDT, *Les sources de l'histoire de France depuis 1789 aux Archives nationales* (Paris, 1907); and for general bibliography, L. VILLAT, *La Révolution et l'Empire*, vol. I, *Les Assemblées révolutionnaires* (1789-1799), in the Collection Clio (Paris: Les Presses Universitaires, 1936). For the parliamentary debates see the reprint of the *Moniteur* (which is an ordinary newspaper and not an official document), vols. XXI-XXV, and BUCHEZ & ROUX, *Histoire parlementaire de la Révolution française*, vol. XXXVI. The most important laws and decrees will be found in DUVERGIER, *Collection des lois et décrets*, vol. VII-VIII; the decrees of the Committee of Public Safety in the collection of AULARD, vols. XV-XXVI; a selection of police reports and newspaper extracts in A. AULARD, *Paris pendant la réaction thermidorienne et sous le Directoire*, 5 vols., 1898-1902 (A collection of documents relating to the history of Paris during the Revolution).

Memoirs which may be usefully consulted include those of BARRAS, 4 vols. (1895-1896), LAREVELLIÈRE-LEPEAUX (1895), DURAND DE MAILLANE (1825, Collection Berville and Barrière); and above all THIBAUDEAU, 2 vols. (1824, same collection); LACRETELLE, *Dix années d'épreuves pendant la Révolution* (1842); DUVAL, *Souvenirs thermidoriens*, 2 vols. (1844); TISSOT, *Souvenirs de prairial* (Year VIII); FRÉRON, *Mémoire historique sur la réaction royale et sur les massacres du Midi* (1824; Collection

Berville & Barrière); H. MEISTER, *Souvenirs d'un voyage à Paris en 1795* (Paris, 1910; Collection de la Société d'histoire contemporaine); *Correspondance inédite du conventionnel Rovère avec Goupilleau de Montaigu en mission dans le midi après la Terreur, 1794-1795* (published by M. Jouve & M. Giraud, 1908).

GENERAL HISTORY

SCIOUT, *Le Directoire* (begins at the ninth of Thermidor), 4 vols. (Paris, 1895-1897, vol. I); G. DEVILLE, *Thermidore et Directoire* (vol. V of *L'Histoire socialiste*, 1904); G. PARISET, vol. II of *L'Histoire de France contemporaine*, published under the direction of E. LAVISSE (Paris, Hachette, 1920); A. AULARD, *Histoire politique de la Révolution française* (Paris: A. Colin, 1901; 5th ed., 1921); A. MATHIEZ, *La réaction thermidorienne* (Paris: A. Colin, 1929); G. LEFEBVRE, *La Révolution française* (vol. XIII of the Collection *Peuples et civilisations*, Paris: P.U.F., 1957).

On the institutions of France, see: J. GODECHOT, *Les institutions de la France sous la Révolution et l'Empire* (in the Collection *Histoire des Institutions*, Paris: P.U.F., 1951); On one particular point, see M. BOULOISEAU, "Les comités de surveillance d'arrondissement de Paris sous la réaction thermidorienne" (*Annales historiques de la Révolution française*, 1933-1936).

On the *journées* of Germinal and Prairial, the bibliography, which for a long time consisted solely of the account of the first Prairial in F. THÉNARD & R. GUYOT, *Le conventionnel Goujon* (Paris, 1908), has been enriched by some comprehensive studies: R. COBB & G. RUDÉ, "Le dernier mouvement populaire de la Révolution à Paris," "Les journées de germinal et prairial an III" (*Revue historique*, October–December, 1955), and above all: E. TARLÉ, *Germinal et Prairial* (Moscow: Foreign Language Publications, 1959); K. D. RONNESSON, *La défaite des sans-culottes, Mouvement populaire et réaction bourgeoise en l'an III* (Oslo & Paris, 1959). See also: G. RUDÉ, *The Crowd in the French Revolution* (Oxford: Clarendon Press, 1959), particularly Chapter X, "Germinal-Prairial"; and A. GALANTE GARRONE, *Gilbert Romme, Storia di un rivoluzionario* (Torino:

Guilio Einaudi, 1959). On the Germinal disturbances in the departments, see particularly: R. COBB, "Les journées de germinal an III dans la zone de ravitaillement de Paris" (*Annales de Normandie*, October–December, 1955); "Une émeute de la faim dans la banlieue rouennaise, Les journées des 13, 14 et 15 germinal an III à Sotteville-lès-Rouen" (*ibid.*, May, 1956). On the repression which followed the *journées*, see: R. COBB, "Note sur la répression contre le personnel sans-culotte de 1795 à 1801" (*Annales historiques de la Révolution française*, 1954, p. 23-49).

THE WHITE TERROR

See works of local history and a few special studies such as: P. VAILLANDET, *Les débuts de la Terreur blanche en Vaucluse* (*Annales historiques de la Révolution française*, 1928); *Le Procès des juges de la Commission révolutionnaire d'Orange* (*ibid.*, 1929); E. COURCELLE, *La Réaction thermidorienne dans le district de Melun* (*ibid.*, 1930); G. LAURENT, *J.-B. Armonville* (a member of the Convention from Reims) (*ibid.*, 1924) *L'insurrection du 1er prairial an III et la situation économique de la ville de Reims* (*ibid.*, 1927); S. BLUM, *La mission d'Albert dans la Marne en l'an III* (*La Révolution française*, 1903, vol. XLV); É. POUPÉ, *La répression de la révolte terroriste de Toulon* (*Comité des Travaux historiques*, 1924, vol. X). For Lyons, see: E. HERRIOT, *Lyon n'est plus*, vol. IV, "La Réaction" (Paris, Hachette, 1940); but this exclusively political study stops at the autumn of 1794. See therefore: RENÉE FUOC, *La réaction thermidorienne à Lyon* (1795) (Lyons, 1957). The examination of the judicial archives remains to be done, except in the case of those in the registry at Coutances: E. SAROT, *Les tribunaux répressifs de la Manche en matière politique pendant la Révolution*, 4 vols. (Paris: Champion, 1881-1882), vol. IV.

THE VENDÉE, THE CHOUANS, QUIBERON

C.-L. CHASSIN, *Les pacifications de l'Ouest*, 3 vols. (Paris, 1896-1899); L. DUBREUIL, *Histoire des insurrections de l'Ouest*, 2 vols. (Paris: Rieder, 1930); E. GABORY, *La Révolution de la Vendée*, 3 vols. (Paris, 1925-1928), vol. III; T. DE CLOSMADEUC, *Quiberon* (Paris, 1898).

FINANCIAL AND ECONOMIC HISTORY

M. MARION, *Histoire financière de la France depuis 1715* (Paris: Rousseau, 1921), vol. III; J. MORINI-COMBY, *Les assignats, révolution et inflation* (Paris, 1925); S. E. HARRIS, *The Assignats* (Cambridge, Mass.: Harvard University Press, 1930); G. LEFEBVRE, *Documents relatifs à l'histoire des subsistances dans le district de Bergues*, 2 vols. (Lille: Robbe & Marquant; Paris: Leroux, 1913-1921; Publication de la Commission d'histoire économique de la Révolution), Introduction; *Les paysans du Nord pendant la Révolution française* (Lille: Marquant; Paris: Rieder, 1924); J. STERN, *Le mari de Mlle Lange: M. J. Simons* (Paris: Plon, 1933); GASTON MARTIN, *La vie bourgeoise à Nantes sous la Convention d'après le livre de comptes de Mme Hummel* (*La Révolution française*, 1933); R. COBB, "Les disettes de l'an II et de l'an III dans le district de Mantes et la vallée de la Basse Seine" (*Mémoires de la Fédération des Sociétés historiques et archéologiques de Paris et de l'Ile-de-France*; Paris, 1954); "Disette et moralité, La crise de l'an III et l'an IV à Rouen" (*Annales de Normandie*, October–December, 1956). On the state of the army, see: H. BOURDEAU, *Les armées du Rhin au début du Directoire* (Paris, 1902); F. VERMALE, "La désertion dans l'armée des Alpes après le 9 thermidor" (*Annales Révolutionnaires*, 1913, pp. 506-16 and 643-57).

RELIGIOUS HISTORY

A. AULARD, *Histoire politique de la Révolution*, *op. cit.*; P. DE LA GORCE, *Histoire religieuse de la Révolution française* (Paris: Plon, 1921), vol. IV; A. MATHIEZ, *Le régime légal des cultes sous la première séparation*, in *La Révolution et l'Église* (Paris, 1910), and the numerous local studies of religious history. See in particular: ABBÉ J. BOUSSOULADE, *L'église de Paris du 9 thermidor au Concordat* (Paris, 1950).

EDUCATION

A. TROUX, *L'École centrale du Doubs à Besancon* (Paris: Alcan, 1926; with a bibliography on the central schools); for the Convention's institutions, see the bibliography of PARISET, *op. cit.*; on society: E. & J. DE GONCOURT, *Histoire de la société fran-*

çaise sous la Révolution (Paris, 1854; 3rd ed., 1888); J. Turquan, *La citoyenne Tallien* (1898); R. Arnaud, *Le fils de Fréron* (1909).

CONSTITUTION OF YEAR III

M. Deslandres, *Histoire constitutionnelle de la France de 1789 à 1870*, 2 vols. (Paris: A. Colin, 1932), vol. I; A. Lajusan, *Le plébiscite de l'an III* (*La Révolution française*, 1911), vol. LX; H. Zivy, *Le 13 vendémiaire an IV* (1898; Bibliothèque de la Faculté des Lettres de Paris); M. Dessal, "La révolte de Dreux et les origines du 13 vendémiaire" (*Bulletin de la Société d'Histoire moderne*, January–February, 1957, p. 5); G. Rudé, "Les sans-culottes parisiennes et les journées de vendémiaire an IV" (*Annales historiques de la Révolution française*, 1959, pp. 332-46).

On the question of Louis XVII there exists a vast and often totally uncritical literature. See the bibliography of G. Pariset, *op. cit.* As far as recent studies are concerned, in one of the articles gathered together under the title *Énigmes du temps passé*, vol. I (Paris, 1944), L. Hastier has elucidated the problem of the registration of the death; in another work, *La double mort de Louis XVII* (Paris, 1951), the same author concludes that the little prince died in January, 1794. On this same problem, see: M. Garçon, *Louis XVII ou la fausse énigme* (Paris, 1952); L. Hastier, *Nouvelles révélations sur Louis XVII* (Paris, 1954).

FOREIGN POLICY

A. Sorel, *L'Europe et la Révolution française* (Paris, 1892), vol. IV; H. von Sybel, *Geschichte der Revolutionszeit* (Düsseldorf, 1853-1879), translated into French by Mlle Dosquet, 6 vols. (Paris, 1869-1887); L. Legrand, *La Révolution française en Hollande* (Paris, 1894); J. B. Manger, *Recherches sur les relations économiques de la France et de la Hollande pendant la Révolution française* (Paris: Champion, 1923).

GEORGES LEFEBVRE was born in France in 1874. At the age of fifty, he began his extensive publication on the French Revolution with a dissertation submitted for the degree of *docteur ès lettres*. It consisted of four volumes on the rural sociology of the Department du Nord before and during the Revolution and was perhaps the longest doctoral dissertation ever written. Until his death in 1959, M. Lefebvre was Professor Emeritus of the History of the French Revolution at the University of Paris. His *Coming of the French Revolution*, first published in English in 1947 and now available in the Vintage paperback series, has become one of the most distinguished contributions to history written in the twentieth century.

VINTAGE HISTORY—AMERICAN

A free catalogue of VINTAGE BOOKS *will be sent at your request. Write to* Vintage Books, 457 Madison Avenue, New York, New York 10022.

VINTAGE HISTORY AND CRITICISM OF
LITERATURE, MUSIC, AND ART

VINTAGE WORKS OF SCIENCE
AND PSYCHOLOGY

A free catalogue of VINTAGE BOOKS *will be sent at your request. Write to* Vintage Books, 457 Madison Avenue, New York, New York 10022.

A free catalogue of VINTAGE BOOKS *will be sent at your request. Write to* Vintage Books, 457 Madison Avenue, New York, New York 10022.

VINTAGE BIOGRAPHY AND AUTOBIOGRAPHY

A free catalogue of VINTAGE BOOKS *will be sent at your request. Write to* Vintage Books, 457 Madison Avenue, New York, New York 10022.

A free catalogue of VINTAGE BOOKS *will be sent at your request. Write to* Vintage Books, 457 Madison Avenue, New York, New York 10022.